Liberating the Heart

Marie-Louise von Franz, Honorary Patron

**Studies in Jungian Psychology
by Jungian Analysts**

Daryl Sharp, General Editor

Liberating the Heart

Spirituality and
Jungian Psychology

LAWRENCE W. JAFFE

To Edward F. Edinger.
Had I not heard his voice I would not have found my own.

———————————————————

Canadian Cataloguing in Publication Data

Jaffe, Lawrence W., 1931-
    Liberating the heart

(Studies in Jungian psychology by Jungian analysts; 42)

Includes bibliographical references.

ISBN 0-919123-43-0
1. Psychoanalysis and religion.
2. Jung, C.G. (Carl Gustav), 1875-1961.
3. Spirituality.
I. Title.   II. Series.

BF175.4.R44J33 1990   150.19'54   C89-090543-6

INNER CITY BOOKS
Box 1271, Station Q, Toronto, Canada M4T 2P4
Telephone (416) 927-0355

Honorary Patron: Marie-Louise von Franz.
Publisher and General Editor: Daryl Sharp.
Senior Editor: Victoria Cowan.

INNER CITY BOOKS was founded in 1980 to promote the
understanding and practical application of the work of C.G. Jung.

Cover: "Window on Eternity," mandala by C.G. Jung, 1927.
(Courtesy Aniela Jaffé and Franz Jung)

Index by Daryl Sharp

Printed in Canada by Webcom Limited

Contents

See final page for descriptions of other Inner City Books

Acknowledgments

It was Edward F. Edinger whose lectures and writings revealed to me the essence of Jung's psychology. I relied heavily upon Edinger's ideas in the writing of this book.

Many friends and relations made time to review my writings and comment upon them. In particular, I wish to thank James Yandell, Suzy Spradlin, Harold Jaffe, Mary-Helen Burnison, Gareth Hill, Claire Douglas, Covie Silverthorne, Barbara Stevens Sullivan, Claire Allphin.

I am grateful to Aniela Jaffé for her encouragement and her gift of the color slide of Jung's mandala that appears on the cover, and to Franz Jung for permission to use it.

Thanks to Maurice and Beth van Löben Sels and to the Ernst and Eleanor von Löben Sels Scholarship Fund which sponsored the research, and to the members of the Scholarship Committee of the C.G. Jung Institute of San Francisco—Peter Rutter, Shirley Macintosh, Thomas Singer and Millie Fortier—who encouraged me in the project.

*In our modern world, [we] have achieved sexual freedom.
. . . Now comes the much bigger problem: the liberation of the
heart. That is the program of the next fifty years.*
—Marie-Louise von Franz, *The Way of the Dream.*

*As a rule the leading idea of a new religion comes from
the symbolism of the religion that preceded it.
For instance, the leading idea of a new religion to follow
the Christian age would be that everyone is Christ.*
—C.G. Jung, *The Visions Seminars.*

May you be born in an interesting time.
—Ancient Chinese curse.

Introduction

"You must pay attention to me," he urged. "If something happens perhaps you will be able to write the book that I may never get written. The idea is very simple, so simple that if you are not careful you will forget it. It is this—that everyone in the world is Christ and they are all crucified. That's what I want to say. Don't you forget that. Whatever happens, don't you dare let yourself forget."

—Sherwood Anderson, *Winesburg, Ohio.*

My name is Lawrence Jaffe. I have written this book to try to convey Jung's healing message to those who have lost their sense of purpose and "forgotten why man's life should be sacrificial, that is, offered up to an idea greater than himself."[1]

While Jung is often thought of as a psychologist with a mystical bent, a kind of oddball relation of Freud, he can be portrayed more accurately as a seer—literally one who sees. He saw early and precisely the condition of moral and spiritual bankruptcy, soullessness and disorientation into which we have fallen. He saw that we no longer have a myth to guide us, since most modern people no longer feel themselves contained in the Judeo-Christian story. Mythlessness means that we have forgotten the purpose we live for, or, more urgently, the purpose for which we suffer.

All religions recognize that suffering is a given. ("All life is sorrowful," is the first of Buddhism's "four noble truths.") Containment in a living religion imparts meaning to our suffering and courage to endure it. But if we don't know why we suffer, life's challenges easily defeat us.

Jung says we cannot stand a meaningless life and he offers us the myth he discovered and made his own: that our effort to be as con-

---

[1] Jung, "Psychology and Religion," *Psychology and Religion,* CW 11, par. 133. (CW refers throughout to *The Collected Works of C.G. Jung.*)

scious as possible contributes to the evolution of God. The name for this process is individuation, the first essential component of Jung's healing message.

The second essential component of Jung's message is the affirmation of the reality of the psyche. There is a scarcely noticed paradox at the heart of human life: all we have is our subjective experience. No matter what our life can be said to be "objectively," all we can know is our experience of it, good or bad, painful or joyful; that is the introverted or subjective perspective. From the point of view of the outer world, by contrast, one's inner experience is inconsequential. Jung's discovery of the reality of the psyche validates our subjective experience, thus returning meaning to our lives.

The restoration of meaning to our lives is the third essential component of Jung's message. Meaning cannot be found in the objective world, it is wholly subjective. Thus if subjective experience is discredited, as it has been in our day, then the instinctive conviction that our life has meaning is likewise undermined, to our detriment.

The concept of individuation is introduced in chapter one, the reality of the psyche in chapter two and references to the restoration of meaning are scattered throughout the text.

The fourth and final essential component of Jung's message is the affirmation of the feminine principle. What is the feminine? Neither men nor women, it seems, have been successful so far in defining it and this book will be no exception. I think it reigns over a space where, as Rilke said, "no word has ever entered."[2] Having acknowledged that fact, I must yet to talk about it, since words are my only tool.

I do not seek to justify the principles of Jung, Christianity or Judaism. I myself do not adhere to any creed or faith, not even Jungianism, and I am not trying to persuade anyone else to do so. Nor do I proceed linearly, in the manner of a formal essay, setting forth a thesis, marshaling evidence for it, rebutting objections and arriving at a conclusion. Rather I wind through the material and in

---

[2] *Letters to a Young Poet,* p. 4.

this way seek to exemplify the thesis that the coming age will see the enthronement of the feminine principle.

Two characteristics of the feminine are that it progresses by circumambulation (rather than heading directly to the goal) and that it celebrates the body (rather than disparaging it). For the feminine principle, words by themselves are thin; it seeks to embody and live its truth. It concerns itself with life—personal, concrete existence.

Just as Joshua circumambulated Jericho seven times before it fell, my strategy is to state a thesis and then to circle around it. I will illustrate my thoughts with material drawn from Jung's psychology, religion, literature and my experience as a Jungian analyst. My aim is to appeal to the heart as much as to the head—another characteristic of the feminine principle.

The self-references in the book are meant to illustrate and dramatize the concepts, not to suggest any special election of the author. The concepts of depth psychology cannot be grasped adequately by the intellect alone. Only when experienced can they become realities. The quotations, the lyrical phrases, like the personal references, are meant to help the reader "realize" the concepts by involving feeling as well as intellect.

Since I will offer no logical, sequential argument, it may be necessary at times to recall that we are proceeding round and round a central idea, which is that Western civilization is about to move under the rule of a new guiding principle—one that has been neglected in the past.

That new principle has many names. Here and in chapter ten I call it the feminine principle. In other places it is expressed as the Psychological dispensation (chapters one and eleven), God needs man (chapter four), man has a soul and there is a buried treasure in the field (chapter nine), the religion of experience (chapter one), the reality of the psyche (chapter two), meaning (chapter six), or the validity of the inner, subjective world (chapter seven). These different names for the new ruling principle reflect differing aspects of it; no one sentence, no one name, is adequate to characterize what is a new manifestation of God, whom no one can describe.

Naturally all these expressions for the same central truth may generate confusion. Perhaps it is best to approach this book not with the critical intellect alone, but in the way you would approach a book of poetry, allowing the words, images and ideas to sink into your heart. Let them touch and move you, if they will, and wait.

Waiting, too, characterizes the feminine principle, and instinct assists in bringing psychic contents to consciousness. In this world little of enduring value comes to us without a period of gestation. The Great Mother knows, even if our civilization has forgotten, that there lies in our unconscious an ordering capacity which will orient us if we give it time and attention. As Jung liked to say, "The devil can best be beaten by patience, having none himself."[3]

I am trying to describe, or at least point to, a new ruling principle, an emerging God. By definition I cannot be entirely successful in delineating it, because God is something that comprehends us, we cannot comprehend God. The different chapters therefore represent different attempts to describe our new God. Open the book at any point and observe whether some thought or idea strikes a chord that reverberates within you. If so I will have achieved my purpose.

---

[3] *Letters,* vol. 2, p. 298.

1
Individuation

My work will be continued by those who suffer.
—C.G. Jung, *The Wisdom of the Dream.*

A Small Demonstration

A half century ago Jung was capping off what would turn out to be
his final visit to the United States with a lecture to a huge New York
City audience. It included some of his most vociferous critics as well
as many of his staunchest supporters.

Jung was planning to explicate two key but much misunderstood
and maligned concepts of his psychology, the archetypes and the collective unconscious. The lecture (unlike most of his work) was
closely argued, and Jung was undoubtedly hoping to present a cogent and persuasive case. Unfortunately, as a witness notes, "the oc-
casion was not propitious":

> The lecture . . . required slides, a lot of them, and an enthusiastic fol-
> lower had volunteered to project them, but either this man's skills
> were insufficient, or the slides were possessed. They came on upside
> down or reversed, and fell on the floor when he attempted to right
> them. If Jung wanted to see one again, they moved forward, if he
> said to go on, they went back. So Jung stood, pointer in hand, on a
> raised platform before his huge audience, either waiting for the right
> pictures to appear, or hurrying to comment intelligibly upon them
> before they passed on. Meanwhile his adherents suffered. Reacting at
> first with great consideration to the awkwardness of his assistant, his
> remarks became sharper by shades—since negative feelings will
> out—and the suffering of the adherents increased. Yet that misfortu-
> nate lecture ended without anything basically human being de-
> stroyed—not even Jung's relation to the assistant, who admitted the
> justice of a certain irritation. [But] the muddle and all the interrup-
> tions had completely destroyed the continuity of Jung's important

argument. Later he was reported to have told someone: "I was analyzed tonight, if never before." In place of the impressive exposition that he planned, Jung had given a small demonstration. Conceivably this may have influenced the content of what he said later.[1]

Now in what did that "small demonstration" consist? For the witness quoted above it apparently consisted in the triumph of human relationship over power needs, which, if her perception is correct, is as dramatic as it is rare. And that demonstration was surely more convincing and memorable than anything Jung could have said.

In the present age of intellectual inflation words have lost much of their power to persuade. More convincing is the example of a person's life. If one lives a personal truth, and it makes that person a better human being, then that truth may be a worthy one.

In my view, Jung, standing before his huge audience frustrated and mortified and having to "eat it," became an example of his main thesis, that in this age every conscious individual is called upon to live a life resembling Christ's; that is, they must honestly experience the transformative power of defeat or in religious terms live the myth of death and resurrection.

Following the tragicomical lecture, a gala supper party was planned to celebrate the conclusion of Jung's visit. Some of his friends prevailed upon him to say a few final words. Our witness reports that Jung's humbling experience might have influenced his remarks. If so, we owe a debt of gratitude to that inept projectionist, for a more moving statement of Jung's essential vision has not come down to us. Here, in part, is what Jung said:

> Jesus, you know, was a boy born of an unmarried mother. Such a boy is called illegitimate, and there is a prejudice which puts him at a great disadvantage. He suffers from a terrible feeling of inferiority for which he is certain to have to compensate. Hence the temptation of Jesus in the wilderness, in which the kingdom was offered to him. Here he met his worst enemy, the power devil; but he was able to see that, and to refuse. He said, "My kingdom is not of this world."

---

[1] Jane A. Pratt, quoted in William McGuire and R.F.C. Hull, eds., *C.G. Jung Speaking*, p. 94.

But "kingdom" it was, all the same. And you remember that strange incident, the triumphal entry into Jerusalem. The utter failure came at the Crucifixion in the tragic words, "My God, my God, why hast thou forsaken me?" If you want to understand the full tragedy of those words, you must realize what they meant: Christ saw that his whole life, devoted to the truth according to his best conviction, had been a terrible illusion. He had lived it to the full absolutely sincerely, he had made his honest experiment, but it was nevertheless a compensation. But because he had lived so fully and devotedly he won through to the Resurrection body.

We must all do just what Christ did. We must make our experiment. We must make mistakes. We must live out our own vision of life. And there will be error. If you avoid error you do not live; in a sense even it may be said that every life is a mistake, for no one has found the truth. When we live like this we know Christ as a brother, and God indeed becomes man. This sounds like a terrible blasphemy, but not so. For then only can we understand Christ as he would want to be understood, as a fellow man; then only does God become man in ourselves.

This sounds like religion, but it is not. I am speaking just as a philosopher. People sometimes call me a religious leader. I am not that. . . . I attempt only to understand. . . .

And so the last thing I would say to each of you, my friends, is: Carry through your life as well as you can, even if it is based on error, because life has to be undone, and one often gets to truth through error. Then, like Christ, you will have accomplished your experiment. So, be human, seek understanding, seek insight, and make your hypothesis, your philosophy of life. Then we may recognize the Spirit alive in the unconscious of every individual. Then we become brothers of Christ.[2]

In the margin I wrote, next to the following words, "This is the key."

Christ saw that his whole life, devoted to the truth according to his best conviction, had been a terrible illusion. He had lived it to the full absolutely sincerely, he had made his honest experiment, but it was nevertheless a compensation.

---

[2] Ibid., pp. 97-98.

Jung is saying that at the end, Christ saw that His whole life had been a compensation for the overwhelming feelings of inferiority He experienced as an illegitimate child. It is with apprehension that I speak so bluntly. I beg forgiveness of those who are offended by these words but to at least one lonely and forsaken soul, myself, they were redemptive.

That Christ's life was, in a way, a compensation does not in the least diminish Him. No, it draws me to Him and forges an indissoluble bond between us of understanding, admiration, gratitude and love. To interpret Christ psychologically does not reduce or nullify Him. On the contrary, He becomes a living presence in my life. If God is not that, what is religion for?

A major theme of this book, then, is that a psychological understanding revivifies the ancient religious imagery. Thus, scattered throughout the text will be found translations of scriptural passages into psychological or experiential language.

Jesus As My Brother

It was in 1977, aboard a jet bound for Israel (my first and only trip to that homeland of our soul, Jew and Christian alike) that I came across the moving testimony quoted above.

Like many Jews, especially those whose parents or grandparents were immigrants who had survived persecutions, I would habitually experience upon hearing the words "Jesus Christ," a mild but undeniable aversive reaction, like a cold shock. They were words that seemed to say, "You're excluded." Or it was as if I had been born with the memory of generations of my ancestors being torn and tormented in His name. For me to then have a friendly response seemed a terrible betrayal. But this is rationalization; what I experienced was a kind of emotional reflex, and I didn't question it overmuch. And all in an instant as I read Jung's words it was dispelled. I was finally enabled to come to terms with Jesus Christ by understanding Him as Jung said He wanted to be understood, as a brother.

He was one who lived His life absolutely devotedly and sincerely, according to His best convictions only to discover, too late, that it *still* could be understood as a compensation. If that was the experience of the finest, truest man who ever lived, what could I expect? Moreover, the fact that He had preceded me in that fate ennobled my experience and gave me the strength to endure it.

I knew through the writings of Jung and Edward Edinger that this is the destiny of modern man—to live our lives as consciously as we can and to see at the end that it was nevertheless full of error. Living Christ's fate makes all of us God's sons and heirs—this knowledge gave me understanding, which gave me courage. I knew my struggle was meaningful because it resembled Christ's.

Jung As Prophet of a New Religion

Jung says of his message that it sounds like religion, but is not. He claims to be speaking as a philosopher, whereas on other occasions he rejected even that designation, preferring to be considered an empirical scientist. Consistently he rejected the idea that he was a religious leader—an understandable reaction in view of the usual fate of founders of new religions (like Christ): dismemberment and early death.

Jung's protestations notwithstanding, his psychology can be considered a kind of religion; not a traditional religion with an emphasis on dogma, faith and ritual, to be sure, but a new kind of religion—a religion of experience.

The Psychological Dispensation:
A Religion of Experience

Joachim of Flora, the twelfth-century theologian, postulated three periods of world history: the Age of the Law or of the Father; the Age of the Gospel, or of the Son; and the Age of Contemplation or of the

Holy Spirit.[3] In *The Creation of Consciousness,* Edinger explicates a similar idea, which may be paraphrased as follows:

The first or Jewish dispensation was centered on the Law and on a collectivity, that is, the Israelites, a chosen people, the first-born of God and the sacrificed of God.

The second or Christian dispensation was centered on faith and on a single individual conceived of as divine, Jesus Christ the chosen one, the first-born of God and the sacrificed of God.

The third, the new or Psychological dispensation, is centered in personal experience and on each individual considered as partaking of the divine, and on each of us as the chosen one, the first-born of God and the sacrificed of God. In other words we are all of us to be the younger sisters and brothers of Christ who preceded us in living, as devotedly as He could, the will of God. Now the spirit is understood to reside in each of us rather than in the chosen one, Christ. Now we are each of us chosen, the first-born of God, like the Israelites and Christ, and like them consecrated to God, beloved of God and heir to his kingdom. "God is now to be carried experientially by the individual," writes Edinger. "This is what is meant by the continuing incarnation."[4]

As in "Ready, Set . . . Go," or "1, 2 . . . 3," or "thesis, antithesis, synthesis," the third in a series may represent a culmination, a reconciliation or a release of the tension engendered by the first two. Thus the third or Psychological dispensation represents a reconciliation of the first (Hebrew) and second (Christian) dispensations. The Hebrew dispensation is inadequate for modern people because of its admixture of unredeemed darkness, while the Christian dispensation is inadequate because it excludes the darkness. The third (Psychological) dispensation will resolve the conflict by making the darkness conscious through its incarnation in human beings. Humankind is destined to be the vessel in which the darkness of God will be purified.

---

[3] Jung, *Letters,* vol. 2, p. 136n.
[4] *The Creation of Consciousness: Jung's Myth for Modern Man,* p. 90.

The Flight into Egypt

Let us illustrate the idea of the three dispensations. In the following example Edinger is translating into psychological terms the Biblical story of the flight into Egypt. First he reminds us that according to scripture the holy family had to make that journey in order to fulfill Old Testament prophecy:

> When Israel was a child, I loved him.
> And I called my son out of Egypt.[5]

And why is it necessary to fulfill Old Testament prophecy? Because, especially when we are faced with a task that will test us to our limits (which was the situation of Mary, Joseph and the infant Jesus who were fleeing for their lives), we derive much support and encouragement from linking back our current situation to the past, especially the remote past. This process gives our lives a sense of continuity and meaning and gives us strength by connecting us to our roots. It is remarkable the courage people show when they understand the meaning of their struggle.

Edinger writes,

> Christ as an individual figure is made to replace Israel as a nation. In Old Testament usage the nation of Israel is Yahweh's son whom Yahweh rescued from Egyptian bondage. The whole New Testament procedure is to gather up all the sacred contents that have been carried collectively by the nation of Israel and attempt to transfer them to the single individual figure of Christ, the Godman, who then becomes a kind of individual personification of Israel.
>
> If we look at this process psychologically, we can see it as a step towards the individualizing of the archetypal images. The focusing on a single individual figure is a first step away from collective, tribal psychology. (But this remains on the metaphysical level.)
>
> It remains for depth psychology to complete this process of transforming the containers of transpersonal contents that appear first in

---

[5] Hos. 11:1, Matt. 2:15, JB. [Biblical quotations are from the Authorized (King James) Version unless indicated, as follows: RSV—Revised Standard Version; JB—Jerusalem Bible; NEB—New English Bible.]

collective form, later in dogmatic religious form and finally in the
... psychological experience of individuals.[6]

If we experience clearly that we are sons of God we have immense courage for life. Paul puts it in this way:

> Everyone moved by the Spirit is a son of God. The spirit you re-
> ceived is not the spirit of slaves bringing fear into your lives again;
> it is the spirit of sons, and it makes us cry out, "Abba, Father." The
> Spirit himself and our spirit bear united witness that we are children
> of God. And if we are children we are heirs as well! heirs of God and
> coheirs with Christ, sharing his sufferings so as to share his glory.[7]

Like Christ we must make our hypothesis, our philosophy of life,
and live it with utter sincerity. How will we know our hypothesis?
Through the religious attitude.

The Religious Attitude: Careful Consideration

Etymologically, the word religion comes from Latin *religere,* meaning the careful consideration of what comes to us, that is, our experience. This is Jung's departure point,[8] and it explains why he begins
to look (despite his protestations) like the prophet of a new kind of
religion.

Traditional religion posits, "If you believe, you will have the
experience (of God)." Jung turns this around: "If you have the
experience of God or the Self, you will believe, or more precisely
you will know." And how do you have an experience of God? By
paying attention to what comes your way in life, making the assumption that it belongs to you, especially what is negative or takes you
by surprise.

---

[6] "The Christian Archetype," public program, C.G. Jung Institute, San Francisco, 1980; see also Edinger, *The Bible and the Psyche: Individuation Symbolism in the Old Testament,* pp. 14, 42.

[7] Rom. 8:14-17, Jerusalem Bible.

[8] See *Letters,* vol. 2, p. 272; also "On the Nature of the Psyche," *The Structure and Dynamics of the Psyche,* CW 8, par. 427, and "The Psychology of
the Transference," *The Practice of Psychotherapy,* CW 16, par. 395.

Whatever in life shocks or surprises us is likely a part of our own nature which has become split off from awareness and returns into consciousness with an alien or negative face, as most things or people do who have been excluded or repressed. Difficulties in relationships, for example, are a rich source of information about ourselves. But if these difficulties enable us to learn more about ourselves and improve ourselves we will be doing God's work—that is the message of this book.

"Life has gone out of the churches," Jung once said, "and it will never go back. The gods will not reinvest dwellings that once they have left."[9] As its next dwelling place the Holy Spirit appears to have selected the human individual. "It seems to me," wrote Jung, "to be the Holy Spirit's task and charge to reconcile and reunite the opposites in the human individual through a special development of the human soul."[10]

The psychological term for that development is "the transcendent function," which points to the capacity of the psyche to unite conscious and unconscious contents, giving rise to a new attitude.[11] That new attitude, insofar as it represents the assimilation into consciousness of what was formerly unconscious, is the psychological equivalent of the birth of Christ (the incarnation of God).

Jungian or analytical psychology seeks to institute and support the dialogue between conscious and unconscious (the transcendent function) which generates that "special development of the human soul," the incarnation, the realization of the divine being in human life. The transcendent function, notes Jung, "is a natural and spontaneous phenomenon, part of the process of individuation." And he adds these moving words: *"Psychology has no proof that this process does not unfold itself at the instigation of God's will."*[12]

---

9 William McGuire and R.F.C. Hull, *C.G. Jung Speaking,* p. 97.

10 "Letter to Père Lachat," *The Symbolic Life,* CW 18, par. 1553.

11 See Jung, *Psychological Types,* CW 6, par. 828, and "The Transcendent Function," *The Structure and Dynamics of the Psyche,* CW 8.

12 "Letter to Père Lachat," *The Symbolic Life,* CW 18, par. 1554 (italics added); see also below, chapter 4, "How Psychic Change Really Occurs."

Jesus' words, "The kingdom of God is within you," are being realized in our day. Many people must find a relationship to the religious attitude through their own individual experience; they cannot accept dogmatic assertions. As Jung writes,

> Man's relation to God probably has to undergo a certain important change: Instead of the propitiating praise to an unpredictable king or the child's prayer to a loving father, the responsible living and fulfilling of the divine will in us will be our form of worship of and commerce with God.[13]

Depth psychology, supporting the dialogue between conscious and unconscious, can help us to understand and interpret our own experience and live our own hypothesis. To the extent that we can achieve this we make a contribution, however small, toward helping God incarnate in this world.

Experience now supplants faith. Only individual experience is of sufficient weight to counterbalance the dictates of scientism and materialism. These twin Furies continually whisper that the individual is of negligible significance except as part of a group. The idea that there is anything of worth *within* an individual is dismissed. Subjective experience, adjudged now of little value, is equivalent to the stone that the builders rejected which is destined nevertheless to become the cornerstone of the new church—a church of the individual's experience of God incarnating within. This is the momentous task of the coming age, that value and dignity should be restored to the human individual.

---

[13] *Letters,* vol. 2, p. 316.

2

The Reality of the Psyche

In psychological terms, the incarnation of God means individuation. To the extent that one becomes aware of the transpersonal center of the psyche, the Self, and lives out of that awareness, one can be said to incarnating the God-image.
—Edward F. Edinger, *The Creation of Consciousness.*

Jung's Liverpool Dream

If a single sentence could sum up all of Jung's work, it would be this: "Individuation is the ongoing incarnation of God for the purpose of divine transformation."[1] That our human effort to become more aware has an effect on God, Edinger calls "a myth for modern man" who has lost touch with transpersonal meaning. Moreover it is the same as Jung's own myth, of which he had his first inkling with the following dream:

[I found myself] with three younger travelling companions in Liverpool. It was at night, and raining. The air was full of smoke and soot. [We] climbed up from the harbour to the "upper city." It was terribly dark and disagreeable, and we could not understand how anyone could stick it here. We talked about this, and one of my companions said that, remarkably enough, a friend of his had settled here, which astonished everybody. During this conversation we reached a sort of public garden in the middle of the city. The park was square, and in the centre was a lake or large pool. A few street lamps just lit up the pitch darkness, and I could see a little island in the pool. On it there was a single tree, a red-flowering magnolia, which miraculously stood in everlasting sunshine. I noticed that my companions

---

1 Edward F. Edinger, "The Christian Archetype," public program, C.G. Jung Institute, San Francisco, 1980; see also Edinger, *The Bible and the Psyche: Individuation Symbolism in the Old Testament,* p. 11.

had not seen this miracle, whereas I was beginning to understand why the man had settled here.[2]

Jung amplified the dream and described its decisive effect on him as follows:

This dream represented my situation at the time. I can still see the grayish-yellow raincoats, glistening with the wetness of the rain. Everything was extremely unpleasant, black and opaque—just as I felt then. But I had had a vision of unearthly beauty, and that was why I was able to live at all. Liverpool is the "pool of life." The "liver," according to an old view, is the seat of life—that which "makes to live."[3]

[It] brought with it a sense of finality. I saw that there the goal had been revealed. One could not go beyond the center. The center is the goal, and everything is directed toward that center. Through this dream I understood that the self is the principle and archetype of orientation and meaning. Therein lies its healing function. For me, this insight signified an approach to the center and therefore to the goal. Out of it emerged a first inkling of my personal myth.[4]

After this dream I gave up drawing or painting mandalas. The dream depicted the climax of the whole process of development of consciousness. It satisfied me completely, for it gave a total picture of my situation.[5]

Jung's experience reminds me of Jesus' words:

In the world you have tribulation; but be of good cheer. I have overcome the world.[6]

I take these words to mean that when, after defeat and trouble and many years, I am granted an experience of that timeless, still, luminescent center (which for Jung was the magnolia tree bathed in eter-

---

2 "Concerning Mandala Symbolism," *The Archetypes and the Collective Unconscious,* CW 9i, par. 654. Jung's "Window on Eternity" mandala, pictured on the cover of this book, was painted in response to this dream.

3 *Memories, Dreams, Reflections,* p. 198.

4 Ibid., pp. 198-199.

5 Ibid., p. 199.

6 John 16:33, RSV.

nal sunlight) then I will have found a safe harbor, eternally quiet and restful, to which to retire from the vicissitudes of struggle in this world.

Asked to name Jung's most important contribution, C.A. Meier, his long-time friend and collaborator, replied, "The reality of the psyche."[7] That the psyche is as real as the material world, as valuable and as deserving of attention as the material world, serves nicely as a summary of Jung's message. And Jung was indeed referring to the reality of the psyche when, six months before his death, he said,

> I had to understand that I was unable to make the people see what I am after. I am practically alone. There are a few who understand this and that, but almost nobody sees the whole. . . . I have failed in my foremost task: to open people's eyes to the fact that man has a soul and there is a buried treasure in the field and that our religion and philosophy are in a lamentable state.[8]

The Psyche Compensates for the Outer World

Not only is a belief in the reality of the psyche the foundation stone of Jungian psychology, it also represents the stone the builders rejected, destined to become the cornerstone of the new religion—that of the third or Psychological dispensation. Jungian analyst Marie-Louise von Franz began a recent interview by recounting her first experience of the idea of the reality of the psyche:

> I met Jung when I was eighteen, and at that time he told me about a vision that one of his patients had had of being on the moon, and then the man on the moon grabbed her with his black wings and didn't let her go. She was possessed by this black figure, you see. And Jung talked as if this weren't just a vision but actually as if she really *had* been on the moon.
>
> So, having a rational nature, I got irritated and said, "But she wasn't on the real moon. That was just a vision." And Jung looked

---

[7] Personal communication.

[8] Quoted by Gerhard Adler, "Aspects of Jung's Personality and Work," p. 14.

at me seriously and replied, "She *was* on the moon." And I said, "Wait a minute. It can't be. She wasn't up there." I pointed to the sky, and he just looked at me again, penetratingly, and repeated, "She was on the moon." Then I got angry and thought, "Either this man's crazy or I'm stupid." And then I slowly began to realize that Jung meant that what happens psychologically is the *real* reality—I started to comprehend his concept of the reality of the psyche. And that was a big revelation.[9]

Can you think of anything more worthless in the eyes of modern society than an individual human being's subjective experience? Yet on that unlikely, rejected foundation God has chosen to build his temple.

Still the "spirit bloweth where it listeth,"[10] and God incarnating in the soul of the human individual would be in accordance with the primordial tendency of God to appear in the lowliest, most unexpected and underrated place, for instance, as in Christ's birth in a stable, or in the gibe, "Can anything good come out of Nazareth?"[11] God's incarnation in man would lend unprecedented value to something which in our era has been misjudged, the subjective experience of the individual human being.

Looked at psychologically it would make sense for the archetype of wholeness (God or the Self) to manifest in the least expected place because in order for us to become complete, it is precisely that which is neglected which needs to be integrated. It would seem the monumental neglect and devaluation of man's psyche in Western society is about to be rectified.

Jung's redemptive discoveries have the capacity to open our eyes to the hidden, psychic world. As it is written: "The things which are seen are temporal, but the things which are not seen are eternal."[12] Our present society denies the existence and value of the "things which are not seen." And yet the source of man's renewal is pre-

---

9 "Forever Jung," pp. 83-84.
10 John 3:8.
11 John 1:46, RSV.
12 2 Cor. 4:18.

cisely to be found in that realm of the unseen, or, put psychologically, the function of the unconscious is that of compensation. A defeat in the outer world can be converted into a blessing in the inner, as it is written: "The Lord thy God turned the curse into a blessing unto thee, because the Lord thy God loved thee."[13] Or as Jung puts it, *"The experience of the self is always a defeat for the ego."*[14]

The fructifying moisture indispensable for new growth is to be found in the unconscious, the invisible realm:

> And it shall come to pass, if ye shall hearken diligently unto my commandments which I command you this day, to love the Lord your God, and to serve him with all your heart and with all your soul, that I will give you the rain of your land in his due season, the first rain and the latter rain, that thou mayest gather in thy corn, and thy wine, and thine oil.[15]

What this moving passage communicates psychologically is that detached from the unconscious the ego becomes rigid and sterile, while access to the unconscious leads to a renewal of life. The ego (the center of consciousness), because it resembles a spotlight, capable of great clarity shed upon a limited area, tends towards one-sidedness. It requires the compensatory action of the unconscious, which is characterized by diffuse rather than focused awareness and contains within it all possibilities.

The East Acknowledges Psychic Reality

We dimly sense that the East, in its radical immersion in subjectivity, has something to teach us in this respect. But, as Jung points out, in line with the Western motto "everything good is outside," our impulse is to swallow Eastern methods whole, thereby losing the opportunity to make our individual inward journey which alone offers the possibility of a convincing experience of the reality of the psyche.

---

[13] Deut. 23:5.
[14] *Mysterium Coniunctionis,* CW 14, par. 778 (italics in original).
[15] Deut. 11:13-14.

Or as Jung puts it:

> It would be far more to the point to find out whether there exists in the unconscious an introverted tendency similar to that which has become the guiding spiritual principle of the East. . . . If we snatch these things directly from the East, we have merely indulged our Western acquisitiveness, confirming yet again that "everything good is outside," whence it has to be fetched and pumped into our barren souls. It seems to me that we have really learned something from the East when we understand that the psyche contains riches enough without having to be primed from outside. . . . We must get at the Eastern values from within and not from without, seeking them in ourselves, in the unconscious. We shall then discover how great is our fear of the unconscious and how formidable are our resistances. Because of these resistances we doubt the very thing that seems so obvious to the East, namely, the *self-liberating power of the introverted mind.* [16]

The East acknowledges psychic reality. "In the East man is God and redeems himself." [17] Jung foresaw that in the course of the centuries the West would produce its own yoga, that is, find its own indigenous method of coming to grips with psychic reality, and that it would be based on Christianity. [18]

---

[16] "Psychological Commentary on *The Tibetan Book of the Great Liberation,*" *Psychology and Religion*, CW 11, par. 773 (italics in original).
[17] Ibid., par. 768.
[18] See Gerhard Wehr, *Portrait of Jung: An Illustrated Biography*, p. 112.

3

A Union of Science and Religion

Outer world and God are the two primordial experiences and the
one is as great as the other, and both have a thousand names . . . .
The roots of both are unknown. The psyche mirrors both. It is
perhaps the point where they touch.
　　　　　　　　　　—C.G. Jung, *Letters*.

The great poems of heaven and hell have been written, and
the great poem of the earth remains to be written.
　　　　—Wallace Stevens, *New York Times Book Review*.

Depth Psychology and the Bible

It might reasonably be asked why modern-day depth psychology
need concern itself with the Bible. Even if we accept that buried in
the scriptures are nuggets of psychological truth, surely the millennia
that have elapsed since they were first set down have allowed us access to other, greater truths.

Edward Edinger explains that a fundamentally new psychic content can gain admission to consciousness

> only by following a previously established pattern; [therefore] the
> new discoveries of depth psychology can find entry into the modern
> mind (in a truly deep-seated way) only by a reinterpretation of the
> earlier imagery which represents the prior patterns of these new
> truths.[1]

Feeling lies just below the surface, so to speak, of the dried-up
watercourses (the prior patterns). Hence the release of the new spiri-

---

[1] "The Christian Archetype," public program, C.G. Jung Institute, San Francisco, 1980; see also Edinger, *The Bible and the Psyche: Individuation Symbolism in the Old Testament*, p. 11.

tual waters (the new psychological truths) will stir our feelings and revivify our depths.

Biblical imagery speaks directly to the soul of the Westerner. We have grown up with the sacred imagery all about us, but its mysterious power to evoke feelings probably has to do not with conditioning alone but with the very structure of the Western psyche. As the second-century church father Tertullian put it (perhaps overstating the case a bit), "The soul is by nature Christian."[2] This is because our psyche has revealed itself in terms of the Christian myth and centuries of devotion have hallowed it into substantiality.

For the new depth psychological discoveries about the human soul to take root in us, therefore, they must be formulated in terms of the earlier imagery.[3]

Why Jung Uses Religious Terminology

Jung's terminology has been widely criticized as unscientific. But his formulations were addressed to the soul, not just to the intellect, hence Jung intentionally couched his ideas in terms of the earlier (religious) imagery.

> In describing the living processes of the psyche, I deliberately and consciously give preference to a dramatic, mythological way of thinking and speaking because this is not only more expressive but also more exact than an abstract scientific terminology, which is wont to toy with the notion that its theoretic formulations may one fine day be resolved into algebraic equations.

Other psychologists, Jung thought, sometimes resorted to religious imagery, though perhaps not consciously. Jung offered Freud as an example:

> Freud's concept of the "superego" ... is a furtive attempt to smuggle the time-honoured image of Jehovah in the dress of psychologi-

---

[2] *Apologeticus adversus gentes pro Christianis,* xvii, quoted by Jung in *Letters,* vol. 1, p. 392n, and *Psychology and Alchemy,* CW 12, par. 14n.
[3] See above, note 1.

cal theory. For my part, I prefer to call things by the names under which they have always been known.[4]

Jung admits that the validity of a dream interpretation, for instance, cannot be proven scientifically. Rather, he says, its truth is proven by its "intense value for life." He continues,

> And that is what matters in practical treatment: that human beings should get a hold on their own lives, not that the principles by which they live should be proved rationally to be "right."[5]

In attempting to describe psychic processes Jung frequently had recourse to religious imagery. And in examining the religious imagery he noted that in order to imbue it with life it was necessary to understand it psychologically. Thus Jung was building a bridge between religion and science.

> In all too many cases the old language [of traditional religion] is no longer understood, or is understood in the wrong way. If I have to make the meaning of the Christian message intelligible to a patient, I must *translate* it with a commentary. In fact this is one practical aim of my psychology, or rather psychotherapy.[6]

And finally Jung summed up what he was attempting to accomplish in these words:

> To gain an understanding of religious matters, probably all that is left to us today is the psychological approach. That is why I take these thought-forms that have become historically fixed, try to melt them down again and pour them into moulds of immediate experience.[7]

If we interpret these "thought-forms" as corresponding to the traditional religions, this statement could stand as a motto for Jung's work as a whole. As he noted in a letter to a cleric,

---

[4] "Freud and Jung: Contrasts," *Freud and Psychoanalysis*, CW 4, par. 781.
[5] *Two Essays on Analytical Psychology*, CW 7, par. 493.
[6] *Letters*, vol. 2, p. 226.
[7] "Psychology and Religion," *Psychology and Religion*, CW 11, par. 148.

It is my practical experience that psychological understanding immediately revivifies the essential Christian ideas and fills them with the
breath of life. This is because our worldly light, i.e., scientific
knowledge and understanding, coincides with the symbolic statement
of the myth, whereas *previously we were unable to bridge the gulf
between knowing and believing.*[8]

Jung is saying here that a psychological understanding of the
scriptures coincides with our scientific study of the psyche, thus val-
idating both the scriptures and our empirical observations.

The death and resurrection motif, for example, as a myth of transformation, is central both to depth psychotherapy and Christianity.
To understand it concretely (as if one's body will literally die and rise
again) is irreconcilable with science or our modern critical viewpoint.
But if we understand it psychologically we will see that a person in a
depression, for instance, is unconsciously living the archetype of
death and rebirth. Depressed people often try to distract themselves
or pull themselves out of it. But if they do that, the death is not experienced fully and the rebirth part of the process may not occur. They
must recognize that there is a good reason for the depression and that
they can help themselves by trying to understand it.

If they are able to keep a conscious, critical attitude while in their
depressed state (like Jonah in the belly of the whale) they are likely to
experience a fundamental and positive transformation. This is not
what one would logically expect from such unpleasantness, but it is
in accord with the paradoxical laws of the inner world which we
know through, among other things, religion. Thus a knowledge of
the myth of death and resurrection may give us the courage to make
the most of depression.

Because he was so often misunderstood as a religious mystic in
the guise of a psychologist, Jung sometimes shrank from the use of
religious terminology even with some of his patients. A few months
before his death he wrote a letter to one of the co-founders of

---

[8] "Jung and Religious Belief," *The Symbolic Life,* CW 18, par. 1666 (italics added).

Alcoholics Anonymous in which he discussed an alcoholic patient of his who later was instrumental in the founding of A.A. Jung writes that he was unable to talk to the patient in the way he wanted to for fear of being misunderstood. What Jung wanted to say to the patient was that "his craving for alcohol was the equivalent, on a low level, of the spiritual thirst of our being for wholeness; expressed in medieval language: the union with God."[9] And he cites the first verse of Psalm 42: "As the hart panteth after the water brooks, so panteth my soul after thee, O God."

Jung wonders, "How could one formulate such an insight in a language that is not misunderstood in our day?"[10] Jung does not answer his question and I don't have the answer either. But thirty years have passed since Jung wrote those words and our civilization is going through a monumental change in consciousness, so perhaps we can dare to speak again in the medieval language without being misjudged as having lapsed into a pre-rational mode of thinking.

Jung's Psychology as a Union of Science and Religion

Edward F. Edinger has for decades been carrying forward the work that Jung began in melting down those "thought-forms that have become historically fixed" (interpreting the traditional religious images and dogma psychologically) and pouring them into "moulds of immediate experience" (understanding them experientially).

Edinger suggests that we are now entering an era in which science and religion will be united. Arguing that etymology offers us a glimpse of the unconscious background of our thinking, he explains the derivation of the word "consciousness," a concept central to his thesis.

---

[9] "Letter to Bill W.," *Grapevine,* January 1963. I am indebted to Jean Shinoda Bolen for calling my attention to this publication. [Ed. Note: The exchange of letters between Bill W. and Jung is reprinted in Jan Bauer, *Alcoholism and Women: The Background and the Psychology,* pp. 123-127.]

[10] Ibid.

Conscious derives from *con* or *cum,* meaning "with" or "together," and *scire,* "to know" or "to see." It has the same derivation as *conscience.* Thus the root meaning of both consciousness and conscience is "knowing with" or "seeing with" an "other." In contrast, the word science, which also derives from *scire,* means simple knowing, i.e., knowing without "withness." So etymology indicates that the phenomena of consciousness and conscience are somehow related and that the experience of consciousness is made up of two factors— "knowing" and "withness." In other words, consciousness is the experience of *knowing together with an other,* that is, in a setting of twoness.[11]

Later Edinger continues his discussion of consciousness:

On the collective level, consciousness is the name for a new supreme value coming to birth in modern man. The pursuit of consciousness, "con-science," unites the goals of the two previous stages of Western history, namely religion and science. Religion (meaning "linking back") has as its essential purpose the maintaining of man's connectedness with God. This corresponds to Eros, the connecting principle, and the "withness" factor of consciousness as "knowing with." Science, on the other hand, boldly gave up the connection with the other and opted instead to pursue an increase in human knowledge. If religion is Self-oriented, science is ego-oriented. Religion is based on Eros, science on Logos. The age now dawning will provide a synthesis for this thesis and antithesis. Religion sought linkage, science sought knowledge. The new worldview will seek *linked knowledge.*[12]

With Eros enthroned beside Logos we can once again contemplate a world in balance. Feeling and the feminine principle will be granted recognition and it will be acknowledged that intellect by itself is insufficient, even dangerous. There will be a growing conviction that a kind of moral sense is an essential element of general intelligence. This fact is illustrated by how scientific discoveries are often made when expectations are disappointed. The true scientist accepts that nature is contradictory and wonders why, while the ordinary person

---

[11] *The Creation of Consciousness,* p. 36.
[12] Ibid., p. 57.

persists in attempting to bend nature to his or her will. Hence moral integrity is an essential ingredient of scientific creativity. One has only to examine the open countenance of Einstein to discern that here was one uncommonly receptive to whatever nature had to say, without regard to whether it suited his preconceptions.

Since the enthronement (at the end of the French Revolution) of Reason as Western civilization's ruling principle, respect for the inner, subjective life, the domain of religion, has been shrinking. We need only monitor our reaction to words such as "soul," "subjective" or "religion" to confirm their disrepute. As traditional religion declined in influence, depth psychology developed—as if humankind could not suffer the loss of a living connection to the inner world.

4
Christ As Model for Individuation

The life of Christ, understood psychologically, represents the vicissitudes of the Self as it undergoes incarnation in an individual ego.
—Edward F. Edinger, *The Christian Archetype.*

Christ . . . is the still living myth of our culture. He is our culture hero, who, regardless of his historical existence, embodies the myth of the divine Primordial Man, the mystic Adam.
—C.G. Jung, *Aion.*

Immaculate Conception

The psychological meaning of Mary's immaculate conception has nothing to do with sex and is independent of gender. It is not a concrete event that occurred once only in time but a psychological event that occurs over and over in a prepared soul. It means that we are healed through recourse to that part of ourselves which has remained uncontaminated by worldly considerations. That is the virgin in each of us, man and woman. It means that a secret part of ourselves (related to that "still, small voice of conscience") has remained pure, that is, true to its original disposition and unmoved by the allurements of the world which so effectively mold thought as well as behavior.

The virgin, as our healing center, is more objective than our ego and adheres more consistently and resolutely to the truth. In that secret chamber of our soul new beginnings are continually being prepared.[1]

---

[1] See Marion Woodman, *The Pregnant Virgin: A Process of Psychological Transformation.*

38

The Nativity

> And she brought forth her first-born son, and wrapped him in swaddling clothes, and laid him in a manger; because there was no room for them in the inn.[2]

Edinger informs us that the familiar Biblical narrative of the Nativity can be understood psychologically as the birth of the Self, that is, the individuation process (the incarnation of God). As it is written, "And the Word became flesh and dwelt among us."[3]

Edinger interprets Christ's birth in a manger among the animals as follows: "Only in the natural-instinctual regions of the psyche is there a place for the birth of the Self."[4] That there was "no room in the inn" tells us that the "more differentiated, more civilized places [in the psyche] don't have any room for the individuation process":

> The birth of the Self is an instinctual process and not a part of a cultural, more differentiated functioning. Thus there is no truth in the frequent misconception that individuation is another form of rarefied spirituality. . . . It is an instinctual process.[5]

Edinger shows through his study of the images surrounding the Nativity that the birth of the Self typically takes place under inauspicious circumstances. The world not only doesn't welcome the birth of the savior (no room at the inn) but is actively hostile to it (e.g., the Massacre of the Innocents).

The word "world" has two references, one outer and one inner. The outer or objective reference is to the so-called real world. This is Caesar's world (or in the Nativity story, Herod's world). This world is governed by the currently dominant principles and it tends to be hostile to new competing principles. Nothing is acceptable that does not immediately grant tangible results according to currently accept-

---

[2] Luke 2:7.
[3] John 1:14, RSV.
[4] "The Christian Archetype," public program, C.G. Jung Institute, San Francisco, 1980; see also *The Christian Archetype: A Jungian Commentary on the Life of Christ*, p. 34.
[5] Ibid.

able criteria. As Jung says "An extraverted consciousness is unable to believe in invisible forces."[6]

The Massacre of the Innocents

The inner or subjective world that has no room for the birth of the Self is the ego, the ruling principle of consciousness. This "old king" is apt to be initially hostile to any new psychic principle that threatens to displace it, that is, replace the old ego attitude with a new one.

The motif of the old king threatened by the birth of a successor—a new ruling principle—is widespread in mythology and religion. Examples are Oedipus's father who ordered his infant son exposed to the elements to prevent him from killing his father as the oracle foretold; Pharaoh who ordered the death of all newborn male Hebrews because he noted and feared the successes of those upstart Hebrews; Jason's father-in-law who assigned Jason tasks which he thought would surely result in his death; and finally, Herod, who, warned of the birth of the Messiah, ordered all male infants in his kingdom to be slaughtered.

That is how the ego, the part of the psyche with which we identify, tends to function. To the immature, insecure ego, all other psychic contents appear strange and disagreeable. The enlightened ego, by contrast, can more readily endure the shock of discovering it is not master in its own house, as Jung said. If the new, previously unconscious psychic contents can be integrated into consciousness, psychic transformation occurs. To make the unconscious conscious is the healing process common to all depth psychologies. The old king, the old ego attitude, is indeed replaced by a new one. But we don't need to identify with any ego attitude. Our essential being is greater than our ego.

---

[6] *Psychological Types,* CW 6, par. 641.

How Psychic Change Really Occurs

Most of us, psychotherapists or not, don't realize how profound psychological change comes about. We fancy that change comes about through active pursuit, through a conscious effort to change an attitude that has been judged faulty. When therapists and patients strive together in this mode they may increase awareness, which is always valid, but the healing itself invariably occurs at a psychic depth hidden to the ego. Moreover, it manifests in unexpected ways—for example a spouse or a child of the patient begins to feel a little lighter—whereas the attempt to change the faulty attitude directly often has little effect.

Jung says that psychic change occurs through the operation of the transcendent function, a homeostatic tendency in the unconscious that aims to balance out the one-sidedness of the conscious attitude. Because the ego is by definition one-sided, the compensatory function of the unconscious is constantly at work. The ego puts blinders on, so to speak, the better to focus on the matter at hand. A mature ego (the achievement of which is a major goal of psychotherapy) is more open to the corrective and balancing influence of the unconscious than the immature ego which is rigidly identified with the conscious attitude.

The healing and balancing work of the transcendent function is assisted by the conscious experience of conflict. Therefore if one wants to change, all one can do is to accept and hold the opposites (which spring from one's deepest nature); it is in the heat of this conflict that psychic transformation occurs.

The religious attitude of reflection, or careful consideration of the conflicts which life offers us, promotes the work of the transcendent function. Thus Jung says of his psychology that it "only helps us to find the way to the religious experience that makes us whole."[7] The purpose of Jung's whole psychology is to make accessible to us that healing power which resides in our unconscious.

---

[7] *Letters,* vol. 2, p. 265.

I have been surprised how even experienced therapists, in assessing others (and perhaps themselves), fall into what I call the "finding the missing side" fallacy. They look for what is undeveloped or not sufficiently conscious in the other's personality and attempt (directly or indirectly) to help the other (say the patient) develop that side. Often the patient is already intellectually aware of what is undeveloped and feels sufficiently mortified about it. What is more helpful is for the person to continue to live in habitual one-sidedness (which is easy and natural) while experiencing as consciously as possible the conflict it engenders (which is more difficult). Therapy can help keep the conflict conscious as well as contain the consequent suffering.

This may be what some psychologists have in mind with their use of "paradoxical intention," whereby patients are advised to exaggerate the very symptom which they have entered therapy to get rid of. A wife who feels she nags too much, for example, is given the assignment of nagging every time she opens her mouth. This idea is similar to William Blake's apothegm, "If the fool would persist in his folly he would become wise,"[8] except that paradoxical intention is morally a bit questionable since it intends secretly to change the behavior, while pretending otherwise. Tricks sometimes work on the unconscious but I think only when the unconscious has already been won over to the side of the ego.

The idea advocated by Jung and Blake is a bit different. It involves a genuine bearing of the burden of one's neurotic symptom and accepting it fully as one's destiny—which is what it usually feels like—albeit an undeserved one. If we can hold and accept our fate, paradoxically it will change—not necessarily what happens to us, but our attitude toward it.

Another thing the ego can do is to try to remain in contact with the unconscious which is constantly generating counterpositions. In this manner conflicts can be dealt with before they turn into symptoms. One way the counterposition in the unconscious can be identified is through dreams. Sleep research has taught us that everybody dreams

---

8 "Proverbs of Hell," in *The Portable Blake*, p. 253.

every night. In fact when people are prevented from dreaming, their functioning is seriously impaired (though they have not had less sleep). Apparently dreams serve a healing function even if not recalled consciously. To facilitate this healing, one must make a conscious effort to remember dreams. Even a single fragment will do. For example: "I dreamt all night but can only remember that X appeared in one of them." Ask yourself what is the first thing you think of when you think of X and that will give you a start.

Sometimes dreams behave like people or animals. If for some time they have not been made to feel welcome, they will cease coming to your door. But if you open the door a crack and show interest in them, they will appear, perhaps a bit shyly at first, but they will come.

Remembering a single fragment of a dream is a good beginning. The next step is to write down whatever you can remember—even if it is one sentence. The time and attention you devote to writing down your dreams signals to the unconscious that you are taking an interest in it and increases the likelihood that it will express itself to you again. You may think of the writing as a kind of meditation, if you wish. Another reason for writing down your dreams is that it is notoriously difficult to remember dreams without recording them on awakening. Trying to understand them, preferably with some objective guidance, would be the final step but any sort of attention you can give them is useful.

Jung offers as an example of the transcendent function Christ's struggle with the devil (the temptation of Christ).[9] The conflict was between Christ's spiritual and power needs. His power needs appeared to him in the form of the devil. The transcendent function, operating unconsciously, brought forth a symbol combining his spiritual and power drives, the idea of the kingdom of heaven. Christ was indeed a king, but his kingdom was not of this world.[10] This

---

[9] See *Letters,* vol. 1, pp. 267-268. The temptation of Christ is described in Matt. 4:1-12.
[10] John 18:36.

was the reconciling symbol which united the logically irreconcilable opposites of spirit and instinct (in this case the instinct for power).

How We Share in Christ's Crucifixion

1) Through having to face our faults

What makes modern people feel crucified is the realization that no matter how hard we struggle, our shortcomings will accompany us and that longed-for feeling of wholeness will continue to elude us. To be mortal means to be limited. Our inability to overcome the reality of our incompleteness is what crucifies us.

Identifying with our ego we take our defeats and failures too much as our personal responsibility. The Christ story tells us that the God who wants to become man suffers because He cannot wholly and in a single moment of earthly time become man. Thus His incarnation (from an earthly perspective, our individuation) is necessarily uneven, lurching, lacking proportion and grace, asymmetrical and sometimes even monstrous and ugly.

Even while writing this chapter I had to learn again what it was to look upon my life and admit that it is full of error. And what then? "Man's sacred mission is correction," says the Kabbalah. The trouble is, one quickly grows accustomed to and then identifies with one's ideas and attitudes, and correcting them causes immense pain. The Nobel prize-winning scientist Paul Dirac once remarked, "The mind expels new ideas as the body rejects foreign proteins." And as Jung has pointed out, "To become acquainted with oneself is a terrible shock."[11]

2) Through having to face our childhood

Particularly powerfully do the ways and the images of the enchanted world of childhood grip us. Can it never be erased, our first imprinting when the world was young? Many, myself included, hope so. In

---

11 *The Visions Seminars,* p. 206.

my inaugural class many years ago at the Jung Institute in San Francisco, the seminar leader reported Freud's notion that the first five years of life determine one's fate. He said if he believed that he would have committed suicide a long time ago. Jung, on the other hand, he told us, thought that our first five years determine our complexes and we have the rest of our lives to try to resolve them.

Edinger says that the memories of childhood enshrine the sacred object. And Jung writes that of all possible spirits the spirits of the parents are the most important. That is to say, there is an unacknowledged religious dimension to our experiences in childhood, and the hold our childhood has over us is due partly to the fact that in our secularized society there is nothing to take the place of the people and things and locales that childhood has sanctified.

As Adam was the first fleshly man, so Jesus was the first spiritual man. He preceded modern man in being compelled to live his life as consciously as possible. And here is the crux of it. Even for him it was a compensation. That is what is nearly unbearable: to live your life as sincerely and devotedly as you can and to see at the end that it was a compensation, that is, incomplete. You meant your life to encompass the whole but you left out so much. Too many important truths unacknowledged. Too many possible lives unlived. Too many erroneous ideas. Too many no's to the right things and too many yes's to the wrong things. It is written, "The truth shall set you free,"[12] but it should be added, "if it doesn't break you." The fact that I had been preceded in this fate by such a noble soul comforted me greatly. "Christ is the inner man who is reached by the path of self-knowledge."[13]

The Christian cross depicts the intersection of vertical and horizontal lines, symbolizing the intersection of the divine and the earthly. Marion Woodman sees in T.S. Eliot's poetic expression, "the intersection of the timeless moment," an image portraying life as a necklace made up of such moments when the divine and the human

---

[12] John 8:32, NEB.
[13] Jung, "Gnostic Symbols of the Self," *Aion*, CW 9ii, par. 318.

intersect.[14] The crucifixion occurred at high noon when the sun, as the symbol of consciousness, was at its zenith. This suggests that consciousness is a necessary condition for reconciling the opposites, which is so essential a part of the process of individuation.

3) Through suffering

According to an Hassidic story, several pious Jews once asked their rabbi about the passage in the Torah that states the fundamental creed of the Jews, the *Shema:*

> Hear O Israel, the Lord our God, the Lord is one Lord; and you shall love the Lord your God with all your heart and with all your soul, and with all your might. And these words which I command you this day shall be upon your heart; and you shall teach them diligently to your children, and shall talk of them when you sit in your house, and when you walk by the way, and when you lie down, and when you rise. And you shall bind them as a sign upon your hand, and they shall be as frontlets between your eyes. And you shall write them on the door-posts of your house and on your gates.[15]

The Jews asked, "Rebbe, Rebbe, why is it written that these words shall be *upon* your heart? Why not rather, *into* your heart?"

The rabbi replied, "Because it is not within the power of man to put those words into his heart. All we can do is lay these words upon our heart so that, when our heart breaks, they can drop in."

Jung renders the same idea in his remark, previously noted, that the experience of the Self is always a defeat for the ego.[16] Or as the Psalms put it: "The Lord is nigh unto them that are of a broken heart; and saveth such as be of a contrite spirit."[17] And: "The sacrifices of God are a broken spirit: a humble and a contrite heart, O God, thou will not despise."[18]

---

[14] *The Pregnant Virgin: A Process of Psychological Transformation,* p. 73.
[15] Deut. 6:5-9, RSV.
[16] *Mysterium Coniunctionis,* CW 14, par. 778.
[17] Ps. 34:18.
[18] Ps. 51:17.

Isaiah speaks of God as dwelling "in the high and holy place, with him also that is of a contrite and humble spirit, to revive the spirit of the humble, and to revive the heart of the contrite ones."[19] Evidently the archetype of wholeness is disposed to constellate in response to adverse circumstances. In this regard, Jung was fond of quoting Hölderlin, "Where danger is, there too the rescuing power grows."[20]

Mary and Martha, Introvert and Extravert:
The Value of Subjectivity

In Luke 10:38 it is recorded that Martha invited Jesus and his disciples to her home:

> And she had a sister called Mary, who sat at the Lord's feet and listened to his teaching. But Martha was distracted with much serving; and she went to him and said, 'Lord, do you not care that my sister has left me to serve alone? Tell her then to help me." But the Lord answered her, "Martha, Martha, you are anxious and troubled about many things; one thing is needful. Mary has chosen the good portion, which shall not be taken away from her." (RSV)

William Blake distinguished two types of men, "the productive" and "the devouring."[21] If we understand Martha and Mary to represent two sides of a single personality, Martha would correspond to the productive, active or extraverted side and Mary to the devouring, receptive or introverted side.

We can understand this Biblical passage as a compensation for our tendency (probably even stronger now than in former times) to emphasize action and doing (Martha) over being and contemplating (Mary). In contrast to this collective attitude (in which even the churches now collude) Christ says that the more introverted (read "subjective") Mary has chosen the good portion.

---

[19] Isa. 57:15

[20] *Memories, Dreams, Reflections*, p. 245; *Letters*, vol. 2, p. 193; *Symbols of Transformation*, CW 5, par. 630 (author's translation).

[21] "The Marriage of Heaven and Hell," in *The Portable Blake*, p. 259.

Some may wonder why Christ was not more supportive of Martha. Psychologically understood, Christ was emphasizing that nothing, not even hospitality, not even a show of consideration for one's sister, was more important than a readiness to receive the God within.

This God within, this "humble, poor God hanging on a cross,"[22] refers to Christ but also to ourselves—not, of course, our selfish, desirous, egocentric self that we are only too aware of, but that secret self that mainly whispers in the silences—the silences which in our increasingly frantic extraversion are more and more infrequent. Christ said, "One thing is needful,"[23] and that thing is to listen to the inner voice and put oneself in touch with the subjective Self—the savior within.

God attempts to correct us, at first gently. As it is written, "A word stole into my ears and they caught the whisper of it."[24] But if we fail to heed those whisperings of the soul, if we do not become more aware of the contents of our unconscious, we may be condemned to live them out. This is what happened to Job.[25] If he had assimilated God's warnings of his hubris which came to him in the "anxious visions of the night,"[26] he might have been able to avoid his terrible fate.

God is always speaking to us if we can only emulate Mary and sit quietly at his feet and listen. But Western civilization, like Martha, is fascinated by the "reality" of the outer world and caught up with its demands. It is surely difficult to say no to those demands, especially in a society such as ours where a goal-oriented mentality unashamedly prevails and value is attributed mainly to deeds, actions and "hard" facts.

---

22 Jung, *The Visions Seminars,* p. 86.

23 Luke 10:42, RSV.

24 Job 4:12, NEB.

25 See Edward F. Edinger, *The Bible and the Psyche: Individuation Symbolism in the Old Testament,* pp. 13-14, and *Encounter with the Self: A Jungian Commentary on William Blake's Illustrations of the Book of Job.*

26 Job 4:13, NEB.

A placement of the highest value on subjective development (compared to which outer reality is considered illusionary) is hard for us to imagine, but an assimilation of that view by Western civilization will, according to Jung, characterize the coming age of the Psychological dispensation.

It was that same introverted Mary who sat rapturously at her Master's feet, oblivious to the demands of the outer situation, who also ran afoul of the disciples:

> Jesus was at Bethany in the house of Simon the leper, when a woman came to him with an alabaster jar of the most expensive ointment, and poured it on his head as he was at table. When they saw this, the disciples were indignant; "Why this waste?" they said. "This could have been sold at a high price and the money given to the poor." Jesus noticed this. "Why do you trouble the woman?" he said to them. "What she has done for me is one of the good works indeed! You have the poor with you always, but you will not always have me. When she poured this ointment on my body, she did it to prepare me for burial. Truly, I say to you, wherever this gospel is preached in the whole world, what she has done will be told in memory of her."[27]

So here too, let us recall Mary. Jesus obviously wanted to honor her deed. Why? First, because He, as the "despised and rejected of men"[28] wanted to emphasize that we must attend to the despised and rejected parts of ourselves because only therein lies salvation, that is, individuation. And second, because the actions of the introverted feeling type (as Mary probably was) are so easily misunderstood and underrated.

Clearly this Mary of Bethany, who appears but three times in all the gospel (two of the verses have been cited above) is worth closer scrutiny. Only once does she speak (in the resurrection of Lazarus narrative) and then only to repeat the remark of her sister Martha, "Lord, if you had been here my brother would not have died."[29] But

[27] Matt. 26:6, JB, RSV.
[28] Isa. 53:3.
[29] John 11:21, RSV.

Mary's tears moved Jesus and a great miracle occurred on that day. Mary's attunement to her inner state seemed always to have great power to influence Jesus. Let us allow ourselves also to fall under her influence.

Returning again to the incident of the anointing at Bethany, we can apply to the Biblical narrative the same method of interpretation that we apply to dreams. Our justification for doing so is that the scriptures can be looked upon as collective dreams, instances when the unconscious, or, in religious terms, God, speaks to us. The interpretive device I have in mind is the understanding that what happens in a narrative is the result of what preceded it. This of course is the logical fallacy *post hoc ergo propter hoc* (after this therefore because of this). While we cannot assume that if rain follows a rain dance it was caused by the rain dance, the unconscious often does follow a "logic" akin to that. (It is another instance of how the laws of the subjective realm differ from those of the objective realm.)

What follows the anointing at Bethany is Judas's betrayal of Jesus for thirty pieces of silver. Perhaps we can view Judas as representing the values of the objective world. Jesus had rebuked the disciples (presumably including Judas) who troubled Mary for wasting the expensive ointment on Jesus, and in return Judas repudiated Jesus. We can take it as axiomatic that the world will reject whatever or whoever rejects the world's values. Money is not only the world's highest value but its very measure of value informing us as to what is desirable, indeed what is permissible. Money keeps the outer world going and in balance. It flows to where the energy wants to go for the next important task. Subjective feeling, as symbolized by Mary of Bethany, performs the same function in the inner world.

It is interesting that Judas, who accused Mary of wasting the ointment which could have been sold to help the poor, is himself called the "son of perdition,"[30] which means waste. It is clear that it all depends on how you view wastefulness. From the point of view of the inner world the pursuit of money and all the energy we pour

---

30 John 17:12.

into the "ten thousand things" of this world are a waste, whereas our extraverted society neglects the inner life and considers it nearly worthless.

An understanding of the following passage hinges on the answer to this question: To whom does the phrase "the least of these my brethren" refer? Whoever it is, it is also Christ, that much is certain. The traditional interpretation is that it refers also to an outer person, perhaps a poor man, and we are once again being reminded to care for our neighbor. But however worthy it is to care for the poor or the stranger, there may also be a poor neglected stranger within us.

When the Son of Man comes in his glory, escorted by all the angels, then he will take his seat on his throne of glory. All the nations will be assembled before him and he will separate men one from another as the shepherd separates sheep from goats, and he will place the sheep at his right hand, but the goats at the left. Then the King will say to those on his right hand, "Come, you whom my Father has blessed, inherit the kingdom prepared for you from the foundation of the world; for I was hungry and you gave me meat; I was thirsty and you gave me drink; I was a stranger and you took me in. I was naked and you clothed me, I was sick and you visited me, I was in prison and you came to see me."

Then the virtuous will answer him, "Lord when did we see you hungry and feed you; or thirsty and give you drink? When did we see you a stranger and take you in or naked and clothe you? And when did we see you sick or in prison and visit you?" And the King will answer, "I tell you solemnly, in so far as you did this to one of the least of these my brethren, you did it to me."

Next he will say to those on his left hand, "Go away from me, with your curse upon you, to the eternal fire prepared for the devil and his angels. For I was hungry and you never gave me meat; I was thirsty and you never gave me anything to drink; I was a stranger and you never took me in, naked and you never clothed me, sick and in prison and you never visited me."

Then it will be their turn to ask, "Lord, when did we see you hungry or thirsty, a stranger or naked, sick or in prison, and did not come to your help?" Then he will answer, "I tell you solemnly, in so far as you neglected to do this to one of the least of these, you neglected to do it to me." And they will go away to eternal punishment, and the virtuous to eternal life.[31]

Jung thinks the poorest and most neglected thing is our own psyche, that "the least of these my brethren" is oneself, especially those parts of oneself that are considered unacceptable and which we therefore habitually neglect and depreciate.

Mote in Your Brother's Eye or Beam in Your Own?

And why beholdest thou the mote that is in thy brother's eye, but considerest not the beam that is in thine own eye? Or how wilt thou say to thy brother, Let me pull out the mote out of thine eye; and behold a beam is in thine own eye? Thou hypocrite, first cast out the beam out of thine own eye; and then shalt thou see clearly to cast out the mote out of thy brother's eye.[32]

This important passage has suffered from overexposure though surely not from overobservance. Perhaps this tells us something about how urgently we need to hear and understand the message it contains and how difficult we find it to follow.

Jesus' metaphor is a rendering of the psychological mechanism of projection or "unconscious perception."[33] The latter term is preferable because it is more descriptive and also connotes something natural (rather than pathological). This accords with the fact that unconscious perception, or perceiving in others what is also in ourselves, is not a pathological process so long as we proceed to identify how the trait that we see in others exists also in ourselves. Projection, in other words, can lead to self-understanding.

Projection generally refers to seeing in another person or thing a characteristic or attitude that really belongs to ourselves, although we are not aware of it. For example, the conviction that one's partner is ambivalent about the relationship may be so powerful that it com-

---

[31] Matt. 25:31-46, JB, RSV.
[32] Matt. 7:3-5.
[33] See Edward C. Whitmont, *The Symbolic Quest,* pp. 60ff.

pletely obscures one's own ambivalence. More, to suspect the other of infidelity often points to our own unacknowledged desires.

Jung emphasizes that projection is a natural process. He says that everything unconscious is projected. We seldom learn something new about ourselves by directly observing it in our inner landscape. Usually it is only after seeing a particular trait in another that we can begin to claim it as our own. For instance the awareness gradually dawns on us that we have a great fear of being alone. Normally we would have noticed this first in others—a high school friend, for instance, whom we haven't thought of in years, appears to us in a dream (which comes to us from outside, the non-ego). We ask ourselves what is the first thing that comes to mind about that friend and we think of how afraid she was to be alone. We find that this thought "clicks" or makes sense; that is, it fits into our other associations to the dream and to our present situation. "Yes," we may acknowledge, "I am feeling lonely right now."

Because so much of us remains unconscious we can never cease projecting. What is harmful is not the process of projection per se, but the failure to recognize projections when they are called to our attention. To recognize and withdraw projections is God's work because in so doing we build up our consciousness and discover who we are. As the church father Clement of Alexandria said, "When a man knows himself, he knows God."[34] In addition we release other people from carrying the heavy emotional burden of our misperceptions, misjudgments, misidentifications and distortions.

Of course matters are not as simple as this because our projection often has some truth to it, though it may be more pertinent to oneself than to the other. By pertinent I mean it may be more relevant and timely to our individuation process to be aware that *at this moment,* for example, we have doubts about our relationship with our partner than it is for our partner to examine that issue. The unfolding of our partner's consciousness may at this moment be taking a different direction; thus our projection may be an intrusion upon the other's in-

---

[34] *Paedagogus,* III, 1, quoted by Jung in *Aion,* CW 9ii, par. 347.

dividuation process while for us, because the knowledge of our ambivalence has (in projection) burst upon our consciousness, it must
have some current meaning for our own individuation.

Recognizing projections, disentangling them and sorting out what
belongs to oneself, is terribly important and difficult work. It requires a kind of moral integrity that in some people has been severely
injured by (for example) unfortunate childhood events. These people
may not possess the fortitude, at this juncture in their life, to participate in the task.

The opportunity to disentangle projections is granted most richly
in two contexts, psychotherapy and friendship or marriage. That is
why long-term committed relationships generally contribute more to
individuation than shorter ones. The initial love feelings (positive
projections) must fade for the negative ones to heave into view. It is
the negative projections that usually cause the most trouble though
positive projections may also be difficult to claim as one's own. We
often fall in love with our own potential, which we see in another's
strength, intelligence, grace, beauty, goodness, vulnerability or integrity. Somehow we'd much rather have those traits accompany us
in the form of a helpmeet than see them in ourselves—which may be
just too lonely.

In a sense, of course, we are of the same substance as everything
around us—the plants and animals, the wind and the starry sky—and
so everything we see outside belongs also to our own nature.

When at odds with someone or something, examine yourself as to
your part in the conflict. Perhaps what you become aware of will resemble a mote, but to your brother it may loom like a beam which is
obstructing your vision. Moreover the courage, fairness and good
will you demonstrate in the process of honestly examining yourself
may relieve some of the pressure on your brother, thereby enabling
him possibly to emulate you.

Jesus' admonition to examine yourself applies nicely to unrecon-
structed progressives and other busybodies of which we have more
than our share in these latter days of the Age of Reason. Their
"evident" reasonableness, which sometimes makes it difficult to crit-

icize their schemes on rational grounds alone, is precisely what makes reformers so unconsciously destructive. It is always easy to be reasonable about other people's problems. As Mark Twain put it, "Nothing so needs reforming as other people's habits."[35]

Jesus' statement is also pertinent to current trends in psychotherapy. Led by psychoanalysts like Robert Langs and Harold Searles, as well as some Jungians, increasing recognition is being granted to the role of the therapist's unconscious (that is, the countertransference). Indeed, in the training of psychotherapists, Jung was the first to recognize the primacy of the personal analysis, beside which the importance of technique pales into insignificance. He was fond of quoting the ancient Chinese belief to the effect that the right medicine in the wrong hands will turn out wrong while the wrong medicine in the right hands will turn out right:

> This Chinese saying, unfortunately only too true, stands in sharp contrast to our belief in the "right" method irrespective of the man who applies it. In reality, everything depends on the man and little or nothing on the method. The method is merely the path, the direction taken by a man; the way he acts is the true expression of his nature. If it ceases to be this, the method is nothing more than an affectation, something artificially pieced on, rootless and sapless, serving only the illegitimate goal of self-deception.[36]

Jung urged that the following parable be retold whenever Jungians gathered together, presumably because it captures the essence of Jungian analysis. It was recounted to Jung by his friend Richard Wilhelm, the eminent Chinese scholar and translator of the *I Ching*.

> There was a great drought where Wilhelm lived; for months there had not been a drop of rain and the situation became catastrophic. The Catholics made processions, the Protestants made prayers, and the Chinese burned joss-sticks and shot off guns to frighten away the demons of the drought, but with no result. Finally the Chinese said, "We will fetch the rain-maker." And from another province a dried up

---

[35] *Pudd'nhead Wilson*, in *The Unabridged Mark Twain*, vol. 2, p. 91.
[36] "Commentary on *The Secret of the Golden Flower*," *Alchemical Studies*, CW 13, par. 4.

old man appeared. The only thing he asked for was a quiet little house somewhere, and there he locked himself in for three days. On the fourth day the clouds gathered and there was a great snow-storm at the time of the year when no snow was expected, an unusual amount, and the town was so full of rumours about the wonderful rain-maker that Wilhelm went to ask the man how he did it. In true European fashion he said, "They call you the rain-maker, will you tell me how you made the snow?" And the little Chinese said, "I did not make the snow, I am not responsible." "But what have you done these three days?" "Oh, I can explain that. I come from another country where things are in order. Here they are out of order, they are not as they should be by the ordinance of heaven. Therefore the whole country is not in Tao, and I also am not in the natural order of things because I am in a disordered country. So I had to wait three days until I was back in Tao and then naturally the rain came."[37]

Healing occurs not so much because of what a therapist says or does but because of what he or she *is*. To paraphrase Ralph Waldo Emerson, "What you are speaks so loudly, I can't hear what you say."[38] If the therapist loses sight of the beam in his or her own eye, a bit of integrity is lost. Then, far from helping, the therapist may even harm the patient.

Taoist wisdom as recorded in the *I Ching* counsels us to "set armies marching to chastise one's own city and one's country,"[39] that is, to use our aggressive energies to correct our own attitudes. If we look at our gods (Yahweh, Zeus, Ares, Wotan, etc.) or watch for a moment how we operate, we have to admit our warlike nature. Putting our Ares energy to work against our own outmoded (unconscious) attitudes, habits and assumptions makes the world a safer place for our neighbors and also makes better persons of ourselves.

When we find ourselves wishing to correct others we should try turning those energies inward where may be found, unexpectedly, a readiness of response. To discipline one's own city is good advice when we are anxious to remove the mote in our brother's eye.

---

[37] *Mysterium Coniunctionis,* CW 14, par. 604n.
[38] *Basic Selections from Emerson,* p. 176.
[39] Richard Wilhelm, trans., *The I Ching or Book of Changes,* p. 69.

The ego can reflect on its experience and ask the question, "Who am I that this should have happened to me?" This attitude produces benefits in the eternal world, whereas looking for error in others usually produces no new understanding of ourselves. Neither does it gain friendship or other advantages in this world.

Defeats or disappointments spark a compulsion to improve other people. If one's ego is strong enough to turn frustrated energy back on oneself, the defeat may contribute to psychic transformation. Surely this must be the Christian attitude, sorely needed in this era of nuclear confrontation. But if Christ's dictum that we examine the beam in our own eye before the mote in our brother's does not apply to our brother, disguised in the garb of the enemy, to whom then does it apply? Jung writes these moving words on the subject:

> Only the living presence of the eternal images can lend the human psyche a dignity which makes it morally possible for a man to stand by his own soul, and be convinced that it is worth his while to persevere with it. Only then will he realize that the conflict is *in him,* that the discord and tribulation are his riches, which should not be squandered by attacking others; and that, if fate should exact a debt from him in the form of guilt, it is a debt to himself. Then he will recognize the worth of his psyche, for nobody can owe a debt to a mere nothing. But when he loses his own values he becomes a hungry robber, the wolf, lion, and other ravening beasts which for the alchemists symbolized the appetites that break loose when the black waters of chaos—i.e., the unconsciousness of projection—have swallowed up the king. . . .
>
> If the projected conflict is to be healed, it must return into the psyche of the individual, where it had its unconscious beginnings. He must celebrate a Last Supper with himself, and eat his own flesh and drink his own blood; which means that he must recognize and accept the other in himself. But if he persists in his one-sidedness, the two lions will tear each other to pieces. Is this perhaps the meaning of Christ's teaching, that each must bear his own cross? For if you have to endure yourself, how will you be able to rend others also?[40]

---

[40] *Mysterium Coniunctionis,* CW 14, par. 511.

If, in a conflict, we can admit that we are also at fault, the door to the sanctum of transformation is thrown open; or one could say that the barriers between man and God disappear. Shamed, chastened, guilty, humiliated, one is then in a condition to be redeemed, or to be saved, or, psychologically speaking, to change. As it is written, "Gold is assayed by fire, and the Lord proves men in the furnace of humiliation."[41]

The prophet Jeremiah puts it with great feeling:

"You have disciplined me, I accepted the discipline like a young bull untamed. Bring me back, let me come back, for you are the Lord my God! Yes, I turned away, but have since repented. . . . I was deeply ashamed, covered with confusion; yes, I still bore the disgrace of my youth."[42]

And if by some fortunate circumstance we are able to admit our error, resolving to endure the punishment that archetypally seems to be its unavoidable accompaniment, before too long something in us is likely to rush to our defense, finding it intolerable that we should suffer unjustly. Thomas Carlyle had this to say about our overreadiness to conclude that we are being dealt with unfairly:

Now consider that we have the valuation of our own deserts ourselves. And what a fund of Self-conceit there is in each of us—do you wonder that the balance should so often tip the wrong way? And many a Blockhead cries, "See there, what a payment. Was ever worthy gentleman so used?" I tell thee, Blockhead, it all comes of thy Vanity; of what thou *fanciest* those same deserts of thine to be. Fancy that thou deserves to be hanged (as is most likely) thou wilt feel happiness to be only shot.[43]

Our horror at being subjected to unfair treatment is reflected in our predominant myth, that of Jesus Christ, most virtuous of men, who suffered persecution while still in His mother's womb and unde-

---

[41] Ecclesiasticus 2:5, NEB.

[42] Jer. 31:18-19, JB.

[43] From *Sartor Resartus,* quoted by Edward Edinger in *Ego and Archetype,* p. 61.

servedly died a criminal's death. In between He was misunderstood, betrayed and treated with hostility and derision. For two thousand years we have projected that fate upon Jesus. Now we must take it back upon ourselves.

But who among us would want to emulate Him? Many worthy people in religious life have chosen to live a life in *imitatio Christi*. But it is just as authentic to imitate Christ by picking up one's own cross and living one's own life in this world, taking seriously the world's values (like "success") and struggling to reconcile them with the inner values.

Christ took our sins upon Himself. He showed us the way. We must now carry our own cross. "The Christian cross," writes Jung, "condenses the primordial chaos into the unity of the personality."[44]

Carrying our own cross means, in other words, that we must drink the bitter cup of our shortcomings down to its very dregs. We must accept and face our faults, as minor as they may seem compared to our neighbor's. It is not enough to recognize intellectually that we have shortcomings. In order for psychic transformation to occur, our very bones must feel remorse; our faults then become "a moral problem that challenges the whole ego-personality."[45]

---

[44] *Letters,* vol. 2, p. 388.
[45] Jung, "The Shadow," *Aion,* CW 9ii, par. 14.

5

The Psychological Law of Compensation

Compensation does not run counter to consciousness, but is rather a balancing or supplementing of the conscious orientation.
—C.G. Jung, *Psychological Types*.

There is a crack in everything God has made.
—Ralph Waldo Emerson, "On Compensation."

Everything in Life Has Its Compensation

It is wonderfully liberating when you finally admit into your deepest heart the knowledge that *it doesn't really matter what fate holds in store for you.* For whatever happens to you there is an unconscious compensation. The unconscious evens things out, so to speak. So you might as well do God's will—be happy, humble and good. As it is written, "Do justly . . . love mercy and . . . walk humbly with thy God."[1]

Pierre, the protagonist in *War and Peace,* recalls some of his experiences as a prisoner-of-war:

And now during these last three weeks of the march he had learned still another new, consolatory truth—that nothing in this world is terrible. He had learned that as there is no condition in which man can be happy and entirely free, so there is no condition in which he need be unhappy and lack freedom He learned that suffering and free dom have their limits and those limits are very near together; that the person in a bed of roses with one crumpled petal suffered as keenly as he now, sleeping on the bare damp earth with one side growing chilled while the other was warming; and that when he had put on tight dancing shoes he had suffered just as he did now when he walked with bare feet that were covered with sores—his footgear

---

1 Mic. 6:8.

having long since fallen to pieces. He discovered that when he had married his wife—of his own free will as it had seemed to him—he had been no more free than now when they locked him up at night in a stable.[2]

Jung wrote, "The foremost of all illusions is that anything can ever satisfy anybody."[3] Doing God's will is the closest we can come to achieving what every man desires—to have it all. If we attempt to pry out of life only the desirable portion we evoke also (albeit unintentionally) the undesirable. As Emerson observes:

> The ingenuity of man has always been dedicated to the solution of one problem, how to detach the sensual sweet, the sensual strong, the sensual bright, etc., from the moral sweet, the moral deep, the moral fair; that is . . . to get a *one end* without an *other end.* The soul says, "Eat;" the body would feast. The soul says, "The man and woman shall be one flesh and one soul;" the body would join the flesh only. The soul says, "Have dominion over all things to the ends of virtue;" the body would have the power over things to its own ends.[4]

Even for the outcast, one of life's harshest fates, Emerson has detected a hidden compensation:

> Has he a defect of temper that unfits him to live in society? Thereby he is driven to entertain himself alone and acquire habits of self-help; and thus, like the wounded oyster, he mends his shell with pearl.[5]

Consider the following:

> For anyone who has shall be given more, and he will have more than enough; but from anyone who has not, even what he has will be taken away.[6]

Though it may sound cruel, this passage states the ruling principle in both the inner and the outer worlds. Whatever a man wants with

---

2 Leo Tolstoy, *War and Peace,* book 14, chapter 12.
3 "Foreword to Suzuki's *Introduction to Zen Buddhism,*" CW 11, par. 905.
4 "On Compensation," in *Essays,* p. 101.
5 Ibid., p. 113.
6 Matt. 13:12, JB.

his whole soul, that he shall have, but he will have to pay the price in the other world. As Emerson says, "In nature nothing can be given, all things are sold."[7]

If it is possessions a man desires above all, he will likely succeed. But he will probably have to sacrifice something in his relationship to the inner world, as it is written, "It is easier for a camel to go through the eye of a needle than for a rich man to enter the kingdom of God."[8]

Because the rich man is fulfilled in this world he has insufficient motivation to seek access to another. The rich man is one who is adapted to outer conditions or to the collective. His symbiosis with the collective lulls him into a psychic state that mitigates against being in touch with those inner conditions which would tend to contradict or compensate for the principles which guide him so profitably in his outer functioning. If one is fulfilled in the outer world there is no reason for change or repentance.

Poverty and failure turn the heart toward the inner way. That is why Christ blesses the poor and the meek and reassures the hated and the scorned. The compensation in the inner world is no less real because it is invisible. Jesus says,

> Blessed are the poor in spirit,
> for theirs is the kingdom of heaven.
> Blessed are those who mourn,
> for they shall be comforted.
> Blessed are the meek,
> for they shall inherit the earth.
> Blessed are those who hunger and thirst
> for righteousness,
> for they shall be satisfied.
> Blessed are the merciful,
> for they shall obtain mercy.
> Blessed are the pure in heart,
> for they shall see God.
> Blessed are the peacemakers,

---

[7] "On Compensation," in *Essays,* p. 104.
[8] Matt. 19:24, RSV.

for they shall be called sons of God.
Blessed are those who are persecuted
for righteousness' sake,
for theirs is the kingdom of heaven.
Blessed are you when men revile you
and persecute you and utter all kinds of evil
against you falsely on my account. Rejoice and be glad,
for your reward is great in heaven,
for so men persecuted the prophets who were before you.[9]

A Personal Example

On the other hand.[10]

One day as I was rewriting this sentence, "We have forgotten why man's life should be sacrificial," which so movingly illuminates the cause of Western man's spiritual atrophy, I inadvertently substituted "superficial" for "sacrificial."

I laughed and realized then with what gravity and high purpose I sat alone on this fragrant and bright fall morning and thought and wrote while another part of me longed for the outdoors, for "Men's Day" at my tennis club. Though nearly every Saturday for many years I had participated eagerly in the fun and lightness of "Men's Day," I had for some time given it up just because of its triviality. I had more important things to do with my time, I thought. But my unconscious, trickster as it is, reminded me that even superficiality must be given its due.

Through my slip of the pen the unconscious was compensating for my one-sided conscious attitude. This the unconscious does reliably, both to us and for us. I was forced to acknowledge that my ego attitude (of solemn purpose and dedication to writing) was unbalanced. I was being called upon to sacrifice my attitude of high seriousness to its opposite, superficiality.

---

[9] Matt. 5:3-12, RSV. See Edward F. Edinger, *Ego and Archetype,* pp. 136ff, for an illuminating interpretation of the Beatitudes on the subjective level.
[10] Ibsen's last words.

Working at my desk a few days later I thought, "Do I really have to be about God's business? This is Thanksgiving and outside my window the magnolia tree is in bud. Does God really need my help with his latest enantiodromia (the tendency for everything to turn into its opposite)? To me things seem awry and beg for my correction. But have not old men in every age thought the same? And have they not also been right? And wrong too? Knowing this, do I need to continue to be God's tool, God's fool? May I not glorify God by celebrating my last few years on earth with laughter—laughter also at God, for I am released. I can now live happily—each moment."

I am sorry about the Jews—"a Kingdom of priests and a holy nation"[11]—bent on doing God's will and in return . . . well, we all know what the fate of the Jewish people has been. But I'd rather cultivate my garden and laugh at trouble. I think now God can take care of His business. I'm "Gone Fishin'." While it is true that society has forgotten why man's life should be sacrificial, *I* almost forgot why *my* life should to some extent be superficial. This is an example of how the psyche compensates for a one-sided conscious attitude.

Four Scriptural Examples

1) Moses

The Book of Exodus tells us that the day after Moses finally accepted from God his mission to lead the Jews out of Egypt, God tried to kill him. He was saved by his wife Zipporah who performed the sacrifice Moses had neglected to carry out—circumcision (the dedication of one's vital force to a higher purpose) of Moses' first-born son, symbolizing Moses himself.[12]

Thus the ego must submit, even when it has received its mission directly from God's lips. As is so often the case, it was the feminine element in the psyche which was receptive and responded to the de-

---

[11] Ex. 19:6, RSV.
[12] Ex. 4:24-25, RSV.

mands of the Self. (Other examples are Eve's eating of the fruit of the tree of the knowledge of good and evil, and the Annunciation.)

2) Balaam

Scripture records a similar trick that God played on Balaam. In this story the king of the Moabites, who is about to engage Israel in battle, summons the seer Balaam to curse the Israelites. God at first prevents Balaam from going. The king then summons him again. This time God orders him to go but to say only what God puts into his mouth. No sooner does Balaam pack his donkey and set out on his way then the angel of the Lord is dispatched to murder him on the road. His donkey senses danger and saves Balaam's life.[13]

This story is instructive from several angles. One is that it illustrates the ambivalence of the Self and the danger of being on speaking terms with it. Another is that help comes from an unexpected direction, from the feminine side. In the case of Balaam it is the wise she-ass who three times saves the life of her master (for which she is rewarded with blows from his staff), because she has knowledge which Balaam lacks, seer though he is. She symbolizes the instinctive wisdom of the body which we so often devalue and repress. Instead of respecting it we abuse the body and try to force it to do the ego's bidding.

Often the body knows better and if only we could understand her language, our lives and our understanding would be enriched. It appears that it is women, at least in our time, who are more willing to listen respectfully to the secret whisperings of the body.

3) The Rich Young Man

The rich young man asked what he must do to inherit eternal life and Jesus referred him to the Law—obey the Ten Commandments. This had been his custom, averred the young man, from childhood. Jesus said that if he would be perfect, then one thing remained—to dis-

---

[13] Num. 22.

tribute his wealth among the poor and follow him. With this the young man's countenance fell and he went away sadly "for he was a man of great wealth."[14]

Psychologically, giving money to the poor suggests directing attention to the undeveloped parts of our personalities. But what helps us make our way in the world are our adapted functions. We put our best foot forward and keep our inferiorities to ourselves. Society is goal oriented. It rewards neither inferiorities nor even honest working on them unless they be converted into abilities or talents. This does not occur ordinarily. In the usual course of events, what was originally superior in us remains so and the same for our inferiorities. The most we can hope for is that our inferiorities cease to embarrass us. (It must be acknowledged that their redemption raises our self-esteem and along with it our self-confidence, which in turn may cause the world to revise upward its estimation of us.)

Addressing this subject Jung writes, "The individuant has no *a priori* claim to any kind of esteem."[15] The reward for working on ourselves is ordinarily to be found in the inner world alone, in our subjective feelings about ourselves. These feelings could be considered to be of no value or of supreme value depending upon whether one's point of view is extraverted or introverted. The extreme extravert, too, seeks to feel good, but achieves that object indirectly, by obtaining recognition from society. One's subjective state then mirrors this perception by others. Indeed, for some psychologists this constitutes a definition of self-esteem.

Returning to our text: Jesus then speaks of the difficulty for a rich man to enter the kingdom of heaven. Understood psychologically, this means that a turning toward the inner world (an introverting of libido), requires a disengagement from the outer, "real" world. In accordance with the extraverted bias of the West, this must inevitably be felt as a loss.

---

14 Matt. 19:22, JB.
15 "Adaptation, Individuation, Collectivity," *The Symbolic Life*, CW 18, par. 1096.

Jesus says one cannot serve two masters, God and mammon.[16] To take up one's cross and follow the path of inner experience results in a loss of energy for use in the outer world and a consequent neglect of outer reality, for which a price is always extracted.

Over and over in scripture the distinction is drawn between the outer and the inner world, the kingdom of Caesar and the kingdom of God. These worlds are of equal reality and equal validity. But our society has one-sidedly invested the outer world with all value. Therefore the inner world is in a suffering and neglected state, as symbolized by the figure of the sorrowful Christ. In India, a society that traditionally emphasizes the value of the inner life, it is the outer life that is apt to be neglected, as is apparent in the widespread disease, misery and impoverishment.

Riches symbolize worldly acclaim, which usually leads to self-satisfaction rather than to self-examination. It is well known that success can become an obstacle to an artist's future development. (This opposition between success and creativity perhaps explains the persistence of the image of the poor struggling artist.) It is difficulties, defeats and persecutions which seem best to fulfill the conditions for psychic transformation.

From the point of view of the inner world, therefore, we should welcome the experience of being faced with our faults because confronting them opens up our way to heaven. In accordance with the laws of enantiodromia the spirit is bound to flow into that which is empty and poor. Emerson wrote,

> Blame is safer than praise. I hate to be defended in a newspaper. As long as all that is said is said against me, I feel a certain assurance of success. But as soon as honeyed words of praise are spoken for me I feel as one that lies unprotected before his enemies. In general, every evil to which we do not succumb is a benefactor. As the Sandwich Islander believes that the strength and valor of the enemy he kills passes into himself, so we gain the strength of the temptation we resist.[17]

---

[16] Matt. 6:24, Luke 16:13.
[17] "On Compensation," in *Essays,* pp. 113-114.

4) The Birth of Christ (Christmas)

The Messiah, God's anointed, is portrayed by Isaiah as without "form or comeliness . . . despised and rejected by men; a man of sorrows and acquainted with grief."[18] Thus do the opposites draw near one another. An example is the winter solstice, which as the longest and darkest night of the year is at the same time the beginning of the return of the light, because from that point forward the days grow longer and the nights shorter. It is no accident that this darkest night of the year is practically coincident with Christmas, the birth of the Redeemer.

When I hear the statement, "Christmas is a depressing time of year," I reply that it is not Christmas that is depressing, but that it comes at a season of the year when people tend to get depressed. Something in our souls associates winter with death, so Christ's birth on practically the darkest day of the year comes as a needed compensation; its intention (if the unconscious can be spoken of as having intention), being to encourage and comfort us. And from that day forward, in fact, the days begin to lengthen and our spirits to lighten. Christmas, then, represents a kind of enantiodromia.

Christmas customs are meant to compensate for the depression we might otherwise feel in the depth of winter. The evergreen tree, a symbol of life, is brought into our homes and decorated lovingly with cheerful sparkling ornaments which were once, Jung tells us, the sun and the moon and the stars. Thus we are linked back to our roots in the cosmos and soothed as when we look up at the night sky to see the stars in their eternal courses.

We have images of families and friends gathered together around warm fires, sweets and hearty foods prepared by faithful hands, gifts chosen by loving hearts, the tender harmony of human voices singing carols and the sparkling laughter of children. And to those to whom none of those joys are granted, the colored lights of Christmas silently proclaim that *here,* in this place where they brightly glow, the

---

18 Isa. 53:2-4, RSV.

human spirit has prevailed against the darkness. Of course these bright images are only partially successful in dispelling the inner and outer darkness of the season and the reality of our family contacts may leave us feeling disappointed. But if it were not for the holiday it might go even worse with us—this death of our year.

Like the Sabbath and like Yom Kippur, that Sabbath of Sabbaths, Christmas is a time consecrated to God, a time set aside for looking inward. To the extraverted bias of our Western mind this non-activity is depressing. Many will escape into the frantic activity and materialistic festivity which now surround our observance of the birth of Christ.

But if we are true to our natures, we will conserve our energies at this time of year. In fact the name of the Jewish holiday, Chanukah, which like Christmas celebrates the return of the light, comes from Hebrew *Chanu* ("they rested") and *kah* ("25th of the month," of Keslev).

Many find Christmas depressing because it has unpleasant associations with childhood and family. Thus in recalling us to neglected aspects of ourselves, which Jung liked to call our animal tail,[19] Christmas may perform another healing function ("heal" comes from the same root as "whole" and "holy"). Our tail is a part of ourselves and to leave it out of consideration separates us from the fertile ground of our being. Moreover our soul does not permit us to repress our animal side; if we try to, it comes back in symptoms (sometimes in family members), outer events (synchronicity), addictions and inexplicable happenings of all kinds.

Integrating these unwanted aspects of ourselves, which Jung called the shadow, is the principal work of psychotherapy. To be sure, it is often depressing to look at our shadow, but our chance for renewal lies in what we have rejected in ourselves. Moreover, the shadow also has a positive aspect—our unlived potential.

---

19 "The Tavistock Lectures," *The Symbolic Life,* CW 18, par. 168.

6
The Need for Meaning

Man cannot stand a meaningless life.
—C.G. Jung, "Face-to-Face: The BBC Interviews."

Meaning has no objective existence—it arises out of the inner world. Like all subjective experience (with the possible exception of love), it has been devalued in this rationalistic and materialistic age. It is invisible, intangible and cannot be established objectively. All we can say is that in order to live well we need to think our lives have meaning, though we cannot say why this is so. Religion once revealed to us the meaning of our lives. Depth psychology, for some people, now fulfills that role.

To say that our spiritual longings are merely childish wishes, as some do, diminishes us. In the early days, Jung had much in common with Freud but departed from him because Jung maintained that one's need for meaning—including reflection and religion—was a primary instinct, certainly as important as food or sex, and that God was not reducible to a displaced father or mother image.

When my father and my mother forsake me, the Lord will take me up.[1]

Note that the passage reads "when," not "if," meaning our parents always fail us massively and decisively. Why is this so? Because they are limited human beings; and for the same reason we, too, will fail our children. (Incidentally, the experience of being a parent helps us to understand and forgive our parents.)

The scriptural passage says, then, that we are all forsaken children and that the Lord will take us up. This means, psychologically, that the instinct toward wholeness will guide us provided we can make

---

[1] Ps. 27:10.

70

connection with it. How? By careful consideration of our experience, by examining both our outer and our inner experience with a reverent and humble attitude. In other words we can maintain a connection with God, with the Self, with individuation, through a religious attitude. The ritual, dogma, myth and symbolism of traditional religions helped the believer to a religious attitude. In the old dispensation we were taught what to believe and how to act but we were not told *why.*

What we once took on faith we must now come to know through experience. Many today can no longer believe something because some authority, however worthy, tells them they should. They must have a reason. Jung was like that. When he was asked in his eighty-first year if he believed in God he answered, "I don't believe. I know."[2] Having had the experience of God he didn't need to believe in Him.

The Jungian term for God is the Self. What is the Jungian way to the Self? It is a step-by-step process and the attitude appropriate to it is the religious attitude, careful consideration. It is an attitude that extracts meaning from everyday life. (Defeats and disappointments are particularly instructive.) Nothing from outside compels us to find meaning in life, yet we feel better if we think our life is meaningful. We have more strength and more enthusiasm.

The late distinguished Jungian analyst Hildegarde Kirsch wrote in her memoir of Jung, "The most important gift Jung has given to me . . . is the acceptance of suffering as a necessity."[3] My own experience is that if I can understand the inner conditions that led to misfortune then it gains a certain quality of inevitability which makes it more acceptable. But if I don't understand the inner conditions that led to the misfortune, then I cry out (with Cain), "My punishment is greater than I can bear."[4] If my suffering was just a random occurrence, it is almost unbearable.

---

2 "Face-to-Face: The BBC Interviews," p. 166.
3 "Crossing the Ocean," p. 133.
4 Gen. 4:13.

Jung pointed out that the person who finds no meaning in suffering is easily discouraged, whereas if one does find meaning in it, the capacity for suffering becomes immense. And he added, "Meaning makes a great many things endurable—perhaps everything."[5] Elsewhere he wrote that "psychoneurosis must be be understood, ultimately, as the suffering of a soul which has not discovered its meaning."[6]

Science, logic, reason cannot possibly tell us if our lives mean anything or not. The human being could be defined as the organism that transforms experiences into meaning. I would go even further. Evidently we must engage in this process at whatever cost, even unconsciously fomenting wars so that we will have something more important to live for than the satisfaction of our own ego.

The Twentieth Century: A Small Moment in History

For a small moment have I forsaken thee; but with great mercies will I gather thee.[7]

Isaiah's tender words of reconciliation and consolation can be taken as a guide to the spiritual events of the twentieth century.

It was Nietzsche who, at the end of the nineteenth century, declared that God was dead. Evidently modern culture had to forsake its religious heritage, had to withdraw from it emotionally in order to gain sufficient distance to grapple with it intellectually. Thus the first portion of Isaiah's prophecy was fulfilled ("For a small moment have I forsaken thee").

It was Jung who announced the coming rebirth of God, that is, God's incarnation in each of us who is called to live his or her life with the sincerity and devotion that Christ lived His. Thus God and

---

5 *Memories, Dreams, Reflections,* p. 340.
6 "Psychotherapists or the Clergy," *Psychology and Religion,* CW 11, par. 497.
7 Isa. 54:7.

humans will again be reconciled and the second portion of Isaiah's prophecy fulfilled ("But with great mercies shall I gather thee").

And in this last century (which corresponds to the rise of depth psychology) a revolution in human consciousness analogous to the Copernican Revolution has been taking place but in reverse, for while Copernicus taught that we were not the center of the physical universe, depth psychology has legitimized the conviction we could not quite relinquish—that we were, after all, special. It turns out that we are the center of our subjective universe. And here is the important point: that subjective universe is parallel and equal in value and reality to the physical universe. What Copernicus divested us of in the outer realm, Jung has restored to us in the inner. Only to the extent that we attribute value to the psyche, the subjective universe, however, does Jung's achievement enrich us.

The Psyche Is Outside As Well As Inside

We mustn't forget, however, that the psyche is not precisely coextensive with subjectivity. Jung writes:

> The psyche, which we have a tendency to take for a subjective fact, is really a fact that extends outside of us, outside of time, outside of space like children's dreams which are a summary of what will be their life's problem. . . . Our psyche can function as though space did not exist. The psyche can thus be independent of space, of time and of causality. . . .
>
> The archetype is outside of me as well as in me. The psychoid archetype only resembles the psyche: animals, plants, the wind behave like us.[8]

This is what makes us feel one with the universe—the psyche is not just inside of us, it is outside as well; in fact it permeates the cosmos. Through the psyche we are enabled to feel a kinship with animals, plants, even the wind and the stars—not just because we imagine it so but because we are in fact of one substance with them.

---

[8] Ferne Jensen, ed., *C.G. Jung, Emma Jung and Toni Wolff*, pp. 62, 65.

We Are More Than Our Childhood Has Made of Us

In the new dispensation, with the Holy Spirit dwelling among us, the doctrine that our fate is largely determined in the first five years of life will be dispelled, and recognition will be granted to the fact that with God's help we have it in us to begin to change our life at any moment.

The facts of our childhood cannot be changed but those facts, depending on what we make of ourselves, are subject to different interpretations and everything depends on the interpretation. What is past can indeed be changed. To say otherwise is a great and harmful lie. The past looks different, feels different, *is* different, depending on what it leads to. The extraverted attitude would say, "How your life turns out is determined by your childhood." But the reverse is just as true—how your childhood appears is determined by how you turn out.

Was your childhood unhappy? How did your life turn out? Did you surpass your parents in consciousness, thereby vindicating them? If so, your achievement will endure because it has left its mark upon the psyches of your children and your grandchildren; as it is written, "unto the third and fourth generation."9

Consciousness is just as contagious as unconsciousness. The latter is well-recognized. For instance, if a bus driver is sullen and hostile his mood will affect nearly everyone he comes in contact with. On a deeper level the same is true in a family. When that bus driver goes home his sullenness will affect his wife even more than it did his passengers. Or perhaps he was infected with his wife's unconscious hostility in the first place.

On a still deeper level, the unlived lives of the parents will affect the children. Where the parent is deeply unfulfilled and unconscious of that fact (the two usually go together) it will surely affect the children. I often tell guilty parents (is there any other kind?) that the best thing they can do for their children is to fulfill themselves. Why?

9 Num. 14:18; Ex. 20:5, 34:7; Deut. 5:9.

Because consciousness is contagious, particularly among intimates like parents and children.

Suggestion, advice, coercion—none of these will avail to influence our children as much as the example of our lives. What influences others, especially our intimates, on the deepest level is what we are, not so much what we do. Again, to paraphrase Emerson, "What you are speaks so loudly, I can't hear what you say."

The Parable of the Prodigal Son

What you do with your life counts. It affects the present generation, past generations and future generations. It also affects God. Jesus' parable of the prodigal son is relevant in this context.

A man had two sons. One was responsible, stayed at home and worked for his father. The other left his father's house, squandered away his inheritance in debauchery and ended up homeless and starving. In due time he returned to his father to ask for work since he was now poorer and more desperate than the lowliest of his father's servants. His father was so joyful at his son's return that he prepared a grand celebration in his honor, welcoming him with gifts of splendid robes and jewelry. The other, dutiful son, then complained of this unequal treatment to which his father replied, "It was fitting to make merry, and be glad, for this your brother was dead, and is alive; he was lost and is found."[10]

We can be lost all our lives and only return to the path in our last days, but to God this turning is of immense value, more valuable even than if we had never strayed. The compensatory message of religion is that we live not for ourselves alone. How we live our lives affects others, particularly those close to us and, mysteriously, the whole world.

A Zen adage conveys a related message: Even if we achieve satori (self-realization) a moment before our death, so glorious is that moment that it vindicates all our prior struggles and sufferings.

---

[10] Luke 15:11-32, RSV.

What a person is can even influence present and future generations with no direct contact with that person, according to the idea of the Cambridge biologist Rupert Sheldrake. Let me introduce his hypothesis of *morphic resonance* with the well-known story of the hundredth monkey:

Researchers studying a colony of monkeys on a small island in Japan in the fifties would dump sweet potatoes on the shore by the truckload. One day something took place which had never before been observed—a young female monkey took her sweet potato down to the surf where she washed it. This improved the palatability of the food in two ways: agitation in the sea water removed sand and other debris and an appetizing salt taste was added.

The monkey soon taught the washing ritual to her mother, then some playmates. Slowly the idea spread until a small group was doing it. This lasted for a time, the idea catching on by degrees. Then one day, unexpectedly, every member of the colony was washing sweet potatoes in the sea. It was as if a critical mass of monkeys (100?) had to be reached to topple the balance.[11]

Still more astonishing was the fact that soon afterward, on a distant island, abruptly, and in the absence of communication between the colonies of monkeys, all of those monkeys were observed washing their potatoes in the surf.

According to Sheldrake's idea of morphic resonance, the form and behavior of plants and animals can be molded "by the form and behavior of *past* organisms of the same species through direct connections across both *space* and time."[12] Applied to human beings this suggests that increases in our consciousness effect not only those in direct contact with us but potentially all of our species, present and future.

Sheldrake's hypothesis implies that while it is with difficulty that a form or event appears for the first time in history, the likelihood that

---

[11] See Michael Talbot, *Beyond the Quantum,* pp. 72-75.
[12] *A New Science of Life: The Hypothesis of Formative Causation,* back cover.

it will reoccur improves enormously after the effect is once produced. This idea is relevant here because it suggests that changes in the psychic background of humanity can be brought about by small changes in the consciousness of individuals. This change in the psychic background is what is meant by the transformation of God.

An example from the inanimate world is the greater difficulty in crystallizing a chemical for the first time than on subsequent occasions. Once a chemical is crystallized in Australia, say, it is far easier to crystallize it in London even in the absence of communication between the two laboratories. This hypothesis suggests, in part, that nature resists the occurrence of new forms or new events. Once one does occur, however, it is apparently more easily replicated.

The Parable of the Laborers in the Vineyard

In this parable Jesus offers us another illustration of the laws of the Kingdom of Heaven, that is, the subjective realm.

At daybreak a landowner went out and hired a group of men to work in his vineyard offering the usual wage of one denarius. At other intervals during the day he went out and hired more men. When evening came he began to pay them off, starting with those who had been hired last, who had begun work an hour before sunset. Those who had worked the entire day were disappointed when they were paid no more than the agreed-upon wage of one denarius.

"These latecomers have done only one hour's work," they grumbled, "yet you have put them on a level with us, who have sweated the whole day long in the blazing sun!"

The landowner answered them, "My friends, I am not being unjust to you; did we not agree on one denarius? Take your earnings and go. I choose to pay the last-comer as much as I pay you. Have I no right to do what I like with my own? Why be envious because I am generous?"

Jesus concludes, "So the last shall be first and the first last."[13]

---

[13] Matt. 20:1-16.

In other words the laws of the outer, objective realm differ from the laws of the inner, subjective realm. According to the laws of men our victories and our defeats, our gains and losses are all tallied up. But according to the laws of the psyche, if we live an examined life as Christ lived his (even if only in our last days) it is possible to achieve redemption, that is, we can be justified and all our losses wiped out with a single stroke. As it is written, "My vindicator lives."[14]

Near-Death Experiences

Some survivors of clinical death report that a kind of consciousness persists, at least for a time, after all objective signs of life have been extinguished. Certain commonalities have been noted in these reports. For instance, consciousness typically leaves the body and is pulled rapidly through a dark tunnel at the end of which a being of light is encountered. In the presence of this being the person's life is reviewed with a feeling of acceptance and absolution. The feeling tone is positive and often the subject is reluctant to return to the physical body.

Those who have been near death as the result of a suicide attempt, by contrast, uniformly report negative after-life experiences. As one woman expressed it, "If you leave here a tormented soul, you will be a tormented soul over there, too."

Others, not themselves suicides, corroborate that death by one's own hand counts heavily against one, as Jung said. A man who suffered clinical death due to an accident offers this moving testimony:

> [While I was over there] I got the feeling that two things it was completely forbidden for me to do would be to kill myself or to kill another person. . . . If I were to commit suicide, I would be throwing God's gift back in his face. . . . Killing somebody else would be interfering with God's purpose for that individual.[15]

---

[14] Job 19:25, NEB.
[15] Raymond A. Moody, Jr., *Life after Life,* p. 144.

Similarly, Jung observed, "The goal of life is the realization of the self. If you kill yourself you abolish that will of the self that guides you through life to that eventual goal."[16]

Evidently the way we live and the way we die has far-reaching and unpredictable effects. As Jung said, we are not creatures of this moment only, but are of an immense age, and our existence extends in both directions into eternity, toward the past and toward the future. It is a thoughtless rationalistic bias to believe that life ends with physical death.

Jesus distinguishes between God's realm and Caesar's. "Render to Caesar the things that are Caesar's; render to God the things that are God's."[17] Much unnecessary suffering results from confusing these two realms, an example of which is taking laws relevant to the objective world, like causality and normality and applying them to the inner world. While the law of cause and effect holds sway in the outer world, the inner world is governed by the law of synchronicity. This means that the things which happen to us, if we reflect on them, appear to be meaningful; outer events, especially in the presence of significant emotion, are often consistent with inner states of being. From the point of view of the soul, it is as if the outer events had a secret connection with our inner life.

According to the laws of the soul, if you turn back to God, that is, if you again put yourself on the road to individuation, even if it is in the hour of your death (and proximity to death constellates the Self, the God archetype) there will be rejoicing in heaven.

Edinger speaks trenchantly to the same point:

> We are a product of all past generations. We justify that historical sequence by what we're able to do with [our life], or, if we fail, we condemn everything that led up to it.[18]

---

16 *Letters,* vol. 2, p. 25.

17 Mark 12:17.

18 "The Christian Archetype," public program, C.G. Jung Institute, San Francisco, 1980; see also Edinger, *The Christian Archetype: A Jungian Commentary on the Life of Christ,* pp. 109-110.

The Harrowing of Hell

The religious counterpart to that psychological truth, Edinger points out, is Christ's harrowing of hell. This denotes Christ's apocryphal descent into hell during the three days between Good Friday and Easter Sunday, whereby ancient heroes such as Abraham and Moses were enabled to participate in Christ's resurrection.

According to this idea our personal individuation process has the power to redeem our ancestors as well as ourselves. It corresponds to a widespread mythologem as follows: The hero is swallowed by a monster. The darkness in its belly prompts him to light a fire. He gets hungry so he cuts himself a portion of the monster's heart. Ultimately the monster beaches itself. The hero then cuts his way out of his imprisonment, incidentally liberating others who had been swallowed previously.[19]

If we understand the myth as a communication from the unconscious, the hero's success (individuation) results in the redemption of past generations. It is as if the spirits of the dead as well as the unborn were hanging on our every deed, because what we are and do affects not just the present but past and future.[20]

The sun cycle can be understood as a metaphor for the hero's journey. At the summer solstice the sun attains its zenith, then sacrifices itself and begins a descent into the depths where it is reborn at the winter solstice. In the same way the heroic ego confronts the unconscious and, according to the myth, is renewed.

Jung says of this important idea:

> The sun comparison tells us over and over again that the dynamic of the gods is psychic energy. This is our immortality, the link through which man feels inextinguishably one with the continuity of all life. The life of the psyche is the life of mankind. Welling up from the depths of the unconscious, its springs gush forth from the root of the whole human race, since the individual is, biologically

---

[19] L. Frobenius, *Das Zeitalter des Sonnengottes,* cited by Edward F. Edinger, *Melville's Moby-Dick,* p. 36.
[20] Cf. Sheldrake's notion of morphic resonance (above, pp. 76-77).

speaking, only a twig broken off from the mother and trans-
planted.[21]

And God says to Abraham, distressed at having no son as heir,
"Look up to heaven and count the stars if you can. Such will be your
descendents."[22] This has a double implication, first that his descendents will be innumerable and second that his life will have effects in
the "transpersonal archetypal realm."[23]

Today we are all like Abraham, and our names are written in
heaven.

---

[21] *Symbols of Transformation,* CW 5, par. 296.

[22] Gen. 15:5, JB.

[23] Edinger, "Yahweh and Individuation," public program, C.G. Jung Insti-
tute, San Francisco, 1979; see also Edinger, *The Bible and the Psyche:
Individuation Symbolism in the Old Testament,* p. 28, and *The Creation of
Consciousness: Jung's Myth for Modern Man,* p. 24ff.

7
Jung and Mechanistic Science

That is the great problem before us today.
Reason alone no longer suffices.
—C.G Jung, "The Undiscovered Self."

Every human character occurs only once
in the whole history of human beings.
—Isaac Bashevis Singer, *Love and Exile.*

In his last years Jung was preoccupied with the subjects of synchronicity[1] and the incarnation of God in man. Both these ideas have the effect of liberating us from the oppressive and devaluing grip of causality (nineteenth-century science) and materialism. These inform us that we are victims of circumstances and of negligible importance in ourselves.

Science, though it is only a tool, has for the last two hundred years functioned as a god (a supreme value), exacting, as all gods do, worship in its service. Now we are at the point of emerging from an unconscious and conscious subservience to a science inclined to statistical formulations, thereby nullifying the essential quality of uniqueness in each individual.[2] Admittedly science, even in its primarily mechanistic manifestation, stands as a bastion of reason in a time of disorientation. Yet we must be wary of a science whose ma-

---

[1] Synchronicity = simultaneity + meaning. Synchronicity functions in the inner world as cause and effect functions in the outer world. (See Jung, "Synchronicity: An Acausal Connecting Principle," *The Structure and Dynamics of the Psyche,* CW 8)

[2] Henry John Todd, an early nineteenth-century clergyman who edited and revised *Johnson's Dictionary,* defined "unique" as "an affected and useless term of modern times." *(Oxford English Dictionary,* p. 3515) Presumably he was conditioned by the leveling tendency of the French Revolution and the Enlightenment, as are many academic psychologists and scientists today.

terialistic/positivistic bias has come to stand for the denial of the grandeur of the individual.

Jung writes:

> Man is not complete when he lives in a world of statistical truth. He must live in a world where the whole of man, his entire history, is the concern, and that is not merely statistics. It is the expression of what man really is, and what he feels himself to be.
>
> The scientist is always looking for an average. Our natural science makes everything an average, reduces everything to an average; yet the truth is that the carriers of life are individuals, not average numbers. When everything is statistical, all individual qualities are wiped out, and that, of course, is quite unbecoming. In fact, it is unhygienic, because if you wipe out the mythology of a man, his entire historical sequence, he becomes a statistical average, a number; that is, he becomes nothing.[3]

Individuation Versus Normality

Patient after patient speaks to me of the frustration in not being able to be "normal." What a relief to recognize that normality is a statistical concept with no empirical validity. What a relief to realize emotionally as well as cognitively, completely and unconditionally, that there's no such thing—really—*there's no such thing as being normal.* But what a long road it is that leads finally to that realization.

Science may assert that the average or normal stone in a riverbed is of a certain circumference, say four inches. But, as Jung pointed out, you could search and search and never find a stone in that riverbed exactly that size. Normality is an abstraction derived from the study of statistics. It doesn't exist in reality. A patient of mine experienced a profound sense of relief just on hearing Jung's wise and cogent words that for some people "their deepest need is really to be able to lead 'abnormal' lives."[4]

---

[3] Richard I. Evans, ed., *Jung on Elementary Psychology: A Discussion Between C.G. Jung and Richard I. Evans,* p. 153.

[4] "Problems of Modern Psychotherapy," *The Practice of Psychotherapy,* CW 16, par. 161.

Stones don't try to deform themselves into desirable proportions, but sensitive human beings afflicted by mechanistic science are often possessed by the uncontrollable desire to be what they call normal, by which they generally mean just like everyone else. They forget they were meant to be something unprecedented—that what they were meant to be is a mystery that only they, with the help of God, can realize by living their life, including the error inherent in it, with the sincerity and devotion that Christ lived his. Not that one's life need be a model of beauty or of perfection. As Jung writes,

A "complete" life does not consist in a theoretic completeness, but in the fact that one accepts, without reservation, the particular fatal tissue in which one finds oneself embedded, and that one tries to make sense of it or to create a cosmos from the chaotic mess into which one is born.[5]

Joseph Wheelwright, the charismatic cofounder of the Jung Institute of San Francisco, defines individuation as becoming what we have it in us to become. He does not like to speak of becoming whole because, as he explains in his inimitable fashion,

"Whole" suggests that it's something just around the corner on Third St. and when we get there, why then we'll be like a new shiny Ford that's come off the conveyor belt. And I don't think that ever happens.[6]

One's life may resemble more the twisted little apples that Sherwood Anderson describes:

In the fall one walks in the orchards and the ground is hard with frost underfoot. The apples have been taken from the trees by the pickers. They have been put in barrels and shipped to the cities where they will be eaten in apartments that are filled with books, magazines, furniture, and people. On the trees are only a few gnarled apples that the pickers have rejected. . . . One nibbles at them and they are delicious. Into a little round place at the side of the apple has been gathered all of its sweetness. One runs from tree to tree over the frosted

5 *Letters,* vol. 2, p. 171.
6 David Serbin, "In Conversation with Joseph B. Wheelwright," p. 164.

ground picking the gnarled, twisted apples and filling his pockets with them. Only the few know the sweetness of the twisted apples.[7]

In a similar vein Jung writes of the "lordly beauty and the divine completeness of an individuated old oak-tree, or the unique grotesqueness of a cactus." He continues:

Science is only concerned with the average idea of an oak or a horse or man but not with their uniqueness. . . . From the standpoint of science the individual is negligible or a mere curiosity. From the subjective standpoint, however, i.e., from the standpoint of the individual himself, the individual is all-important as he is the carrier of life, and his development and fulfillment are of paramount significance. It is vital for each living being to become its own *entelechia* and to grow into that which it was from the very beginning. This very vital and indispensable need of each living being means very little or nothing from a statistical standpoint, and nobody outside can be seriously interested in the fact that Mr. X is to become a good businessman or that Mrs. Y is to get six children. The individuated human being is just ordinary and therefore almost invisible. . . . He will be all right if he can fulfill himself as he was from the beginning. He will have no need to be exaggerated, hypocritical, neurotic, or any other nuisance. He will be "in modest harmony with nature."[8]

How is this accomplished—to live "in modest harmony with nature," to individuate? The answer is that there are as many paths to this goal as human beings upon the earth, but for each particular human being only *one* path. It is an inner path which the person must follow. In one's outer life a thousand misfortunes may occur. One may choose the wrong mate, never parent a child (or become a parent when one was never intended to be one), choose the wrong vocation or none at all.

Far from being a barrier to individuation these detours are a necessary ingredient of it. There would be no such thing as individuation if there were not roadblocks and detours just as there would be no

---

[7] *Winesburg, Ohio,* p. 36.
[8] *Letters,* vol. 2, pp. 323-324.

such thing as a path were there no wilderness around it. In fact it is their presence which makes individuation possible, as in the medieval labyrinths whose cul de sacs forced the wayfarer to traverse every inch of the labyrinth, and experience every possible wrong turning, before admission was granted to the central mystery.[9]

The path to the goal is an inner path and remains invincible before the vicissitudes of outer events; only death extinguishes hope of progress in this life. So how do we discover our own inner path to find out who we were meant to be?

To this question there is no general answer. The singularity of each of our paths is part of what makes finding it and staying on it so difficult. We have no company and very few guidelines. A story is told of the Knights of the Round Table, that when the Loathly Damsel broke in upon their merrymaking and set them upon the quest for the Holy Grail, the knights thought it a disgrace to embark upon their journey as a group; therefore each sought an entrance into the Dark Forest where none had entered before.

But can no advice be offered on how to find one's unique inner (and outer) path? I will offer some but first a caution. Advice that is generally valid can be poison in a particular case. For instance the Biblical injunction already referred to, to do justly, love mercy and walk humbly with thy God,[10] is good general advice, but poison to a person too identified with conventional norms of goodness and morality. Say a woman is too identified with her husband and family. She may interpret those words to mean she should continue to suppress parts of herself opposed to her role of good wife and mother—parts of herself that must also be permitted to live. For her the Zen sage's advice would be healthier:

> If you meet your father going down the street, kill your father; if you meet your mother going down the street, kill your mother; if you meet the Buddha going down the street, kill the Buddha.

---

9 See Also Carotenuto, *The Vertical Labyrinth: Individuation in Jungian Psychology.*
10 Mic. 6:8.

This means that nothing is so important as your individuation and you must root out attitudes that you took on as a child, unaware, which do not belong to your essential nature. Or as Christ said,

> Do not think that I have come to bring peace on earth; I have not come to bring peace, but a sword. For I have come to set a man against his father and a daughter against her mother, and a daughter-in-law against her mother-in-law; and a man's foes will be those of his own household.[11]

And again,

> If any one comes to me and does not hate his own father and mother and wife and children and brothers and sisters, yes, and even his own life he cannot be my disciple. Whoever does not bear his own cross and come after me, cannot be my disciple.[12]

Christ says he has come not to bring peace but a sword, meaning that if you follow the path of individuation first trodden by Christ your life will not be peaceful. It will be filled with inner turmoil because you will have to use the sword of discrimination to distinguish, for instance, what belongs to you in a relationship and what belongs to your partner. Or you will have to cut through habitual (peaceful) ways of being in order to reveal whether those ways of functioning belong authentically to you or, say, to your parents. Or you may have to question conventional standards, for example the supremacy of the mother-wife role for a woman.

Nothing is so important as to carry your own cross, says Christ. That means the same as finding and following the path of individuation which has been prepared for you from eternity. This is the most difficult path but paradoxically also the easiest because the only one which will allow you to die with the knowledge that you lived out your life through and through.

The generally valid truths offered by religions no longer seem to work so well without reinterpretation, which is the reason for books

---

[11] Matt. 10:34-36, RSV.
[12] Luke 14: 26-27, RSV.

such as this and for psychotherapists. What collective truths, then, *can* be trusted? I will offer some, but bear in mind that they may not apply in your case.

Remember that God wants to incarnate in you. You may think that it is you who desires growth, change or individuation, but the impulse to "discover the place in the world, which for good or ill, [one] is intended to fulfill according to [one's] nature,"[13] comes from something much greater than your ego, namely the Self or God. Another way to say it is that your desire to become who you were destined to be is a powerful instinct which you must find a way to serve. As the apocryphal Gospel of Thomas says,

> If you bring forth what is in you, what you bring forth will save you; if you do not bring forth what is within you, what you do not bring forth will destroy you.[14]

You must give expression to what is most truly yourself. For instance, you may need to write or paint or work in the garden or sail or play tennis or change your profession or love someone even if it makes a fool of you. If you do not discover who you are and give expression to it, this may undermine your health. Cancer, for instance, can result when there is an insurmountable obstacle to individuation, as apparently happened in the case of Jung's father, a minister, who died at age fifty-two because he could not reconcile his faith with science.[15] One could say that Jung spent his life in an attempt to accomplish the task which defeated his father.

Now, how can you serve the individuation process? Which really means, how can you serve God—because becoming yourself is serving God. Do generally valid precepts exist?

Take a Sabbath, a time of rest, once a week even if only for fifteen minutes. Protect this Sabbath from the claims of work, children, spouse, parents and friends. When you enter your free and protected

---

13 Erich Neumann, "Stages of Religious Experience and the Path of Depth Psychology," p. 31.

14 "The Gospel of Thomas," no. 70, in *Nag Hammadi Library*, p. 126.

15 See Barbara Hannah, *Jung: His Life and Work*, p. 63.

space for those minutes try to be open to what comes to you. You can think of it as meditation if you want, or perhaps you will feel the urge to write or paint or draw or dance or think or be sad or be angry or be in nature. Regularity in taking your Sabbath is essential, however, so body and soul will come to anticipate it and depend upon it.

Self-Knowledge Gives Meaning to Life

> Christ is the inner man who is reached by the path of self-knowledge.[16]

Reading the Biblical narrative of Christ's passion and coming upon the words, "Knowing everything that was going to happen to him . . . ,"[17] I wondered, "Why make a point that Jesus knows what will happen to him?" I thought of how knowledge was being emphasized here and how with my patients I emphasize awareness. I often have to assure them that it is through increased awareness that ninety per cent of the task of psychotherapy (that is, psychic transformation) is accomplished.

I can trace back my lifelong obsession with improving myself to my tenth year and it probably goes farther back than that. Evidently I have felt inadequate for a long time. Why? The conclusion I have arrived at is that for a child of religious temperament to be born in America in the middle of the twentieth century must have been a dreadful shock.

As my schoolbooks were fond of proclaiming, we were living in the Industrial Age; we should be grateful for our high standard of living; we were the "Arsenal of Democracy" or else the "Breadbasket of the Western World." History, geography, social studies were celebrations of materiality and reinforced, rather than counterbalanced, the marketplace values of the world outside the classroom. Truly there seemed no place for the spirit.

---

[16] *Aion,* CW 9ii, par. 318.
[17] John 18:4, JB.

I thought too of how I rejected knowledge as a youth and even into middle age. I realized only lately that I was right to reject the type of knowledge purveyed in schools in the middle of the twentieth century. As Jung pointed out, under the impact of the French Enlightenment the spirit has been degraded into mere intellect.[18]

But a knowledge that tells us what is to come is a different order of knowledge. Jesus reassures us that the Holy Spirit will make known the things to come.[19] This was the sort of knowledge I was interested in, but what was taught in schools in my youth concerned itself only with the behavior of physical entities. I dare say my teachers considered it to be pure, untainted by metaphysical influence, but for me it was devoid of meaning. In the last two hundred years we have learned the extent to which we are like machines and like animals. Now it is time to learn we are also like gods.

The Need to Feel Special

Ours has been called the Age of Narcissism, but let us not be too quick to judge it. The incarnation of God in man, like any new-born thing, is apt to be awkward or unadapted at first. It has not yet attained to the dignity of its mature form.

Jung greatly admired the Pueblo Indians' relationship to God which for them was the sun. The Pueblos knew that their prayers helped the sun to rise each morning and that without their help the sun would cease to appear and the world would die. They believed, living in the mountains (on the roof of the world, so to speak), that of all peoples they were closest to God and that their prayers had a direct and immediate effect on God.

And in another way, too, they felt special. The rivers, like themselves, had their source in the mountains, and the rivers, they believed, were the source of all life.

---

[18] See, for instance, *Letters*, vol. 2, p. 468, and *Psychology and Alchemy*, CW 12, par. 178.
[19] John 16:13.

These convictions, Jung thought, gave their life meaning and lent the Pueblos a striking sense of serenity, strength and dignity. Jung felt that modern people suffer greatly from a diminished sense of their own importance. The narcissistic trends we now see all around us can be considered a compensation for the endemic lack of self-esteem felt by many. This has resulted from the loss of a vital connection to that which is more important than the ego, namely a connection with God.

In ages past, when religion was a living experience, God's order reigned all about us and as His children we knew our true worth. But in the interregnum between the announced "death of God" at the beginning of this century and the present beginnings of a recognition of his rebirth in us, we have suffered, as individual human beings, an unprecedented devaluation.

Like those legendary canaries who, because they were acutely sensitive to poisonous fumes, were carted below by miners to give warning of toxic conditions, some of us (partly because of personal history) have been more susceptible to the toxin of worthlessness which is characteristic of our time. A new diagnostic category—narcissistic personality disorders—has been invented to describe such persons, and a new model of psychotherapy, an offshoot of Freudian psychoanalysis, has been formulated by Heinz Kohut and others to treat them.

These "patients" suffer from terrible feelings of unworthiness, cannot accept interpretations and require an enormous amount of appreciation, mirroring and empathy before they can finally appreciate themselves (though even that is saying too much, for they lack a cohesive self for them to appreciate). They have caused a great flutter in the psychotherapeutic community. They put great demands upon the personal integrity of the therapist. They place their trust neither in technique, nor in professional persona. In that way too they are ahead of their time.

The need to feel special, which in an exaggerated form is a symptom of the monumental loss of meaning that characterizes our age, is on the psychological level a need as genuine and basic as food and shelter are on the physical level.

The Bushman greets stranger and friend alike with right hand raised in the universal gesture of peace and the words, "I see you." But modern men and women walk the crowded streets unrecognized and unreceived, no longer feeling at home in the world.

Jung said human beings will not forever suffer their own nullification. There will be a reaction, he said, because "man cannot stand a meaningless life."[20]

An Hassidic story tells us,

> Every person should have two pieces of paper in his or her pocket to draw upon as the occasion demands.
> One piece of paper should say, "I am but dust and ashes." The other should say, "The universe was created for my sake."[21]

Paradoxically, both statements are true. One pertains to the outer world, the other to the inner. Some have readier access to one piece of paper, some to the other. An example of the reality of the inner or subjective world is the real need of every human being to feel special. Even Karl Marx could cry out, "I am nothing and should be everything."[22]

Indeed, sociologists are beginning to recognize that Marxism's appeal arises from its status as a plausible and comprehensive interpretation of the disjointed modern world which (and here is how it grips the unconscious of its adherents) also offers something worth living for, a vision of a kind of paradise on earth.[23] Thus it offers an opportunity to aid suffering humanity through science. This makes an enticing dish not only for the young, intelligent and idealistic but for the true and good and hopeful of all ages. But it is religion in the guise of science. It is what happens when our conscious relationship

---

20 "Face-to-Face: The BBC Interviews," p. 166.
21 See Lois Ruby, *Two Truths in My Pocket* (a children's book).
22 See B. Berger, "Blind Alley or Road to the Truth?" p. 18.
23 Ibid.

to God has been shrouded—God pops up in "isms," as Jung often pointed out.[24]

If we are incapable of feeling that the universe was created for our sake, we deprive ourselves of a measure of joy in our lives as well as losing access to something that could sustain us in adversity.[25] To deny the legitimacy of the desire to feel special is to deny a fundamental need of the soul. But we cannot and will not accept that denial and so our need to feel special takes other avenues to fulfillment. Among these are the desire for wealth and power. But since these things are limited and transitory they cannot fill our hunger for recognition. Thus some become murderers, terrorists or fanatics in a desperate attempt to put meaning into their lives.[26]

We can perhaps learn from the Maoris, who in their art depict only gods, not men, because only the gods are perfect. This is to say that in order to motivate us in our search for wholeness we cannot do without a relationship to that which is perceived to be perfect or complete. Ultimately only a relationship to God, or in psychological terms the Self, can affirm us in an abiding way.

The Subjective Imparts Meaning

Meaning was once implicit in nature. Evidently, in order to achieve a more detached and objective view of the physical universe, we had to forsake for a time our natural tendency to endow the world with meaning. Jung writes:

> The prime and most immediate experience of matter was that it is animated, which for medieval man was self-evident; indeed every

---

[24] See, for instance, "Psychological Commentary on *The Tibetan Book of the Great Liberation,*" *Psychology and Religion,* CW 11, par. 772.

[25] Of course, feeling special may have no direct effect on the outer world, but it does affect our attitude toward ourselves (our self-confidence, for example), which in turn affects how others respond to us.

[26] Roland Barthes said in one of his last seminars, "One must choose between being a terrorist and being an egoist." (Quoted by Roger Shattuck, "Why Not the Best?" in *New York Review of Books,* April 28, 1983, p. 15.)

Mass, every rite of the Church, and the miraculous effect of relics all demonstrated for him this natural and obvious fact. The French Enlightenment and the shattering of the metaphysical view of the world were needed before a scientist like Lavoisier had the courage finally to reach out for the scales.[27]

Historians have largely omitted subjective experience from their histories, concentrating instead on objective events like wars and the succession of rulers. In order to understand ourselves better we need to be able to feel ourselves into the minds of individuals of previous epochs. We must remind ourselves of the experience of our ancestors who lived in a world filled with meaning and therefore unspeakably different from the world we live in. But we cannot endure such reality (mere rationalism and materialism) for long. We yearn to be gripped by something—if not God then sex, money, drugs, alcohol, food, love, hate, war or any of a multitude of principles for which one is willing to die.

The history I learned, while pretending to be objective and partaking of the mystique of science, merely represented the bias of its time, namely that causes of historical change could most profitably be sought in economics; that is, its assumption was that man does indeed live by bread alone. Through modern science's misunderstanding of the spiritual aspect of human existence, a good deal of meaning has been effectively eliminated from history. Is it any wonder that our children won't learn?

The Baneful Effect of Mechanistic Science

Academic psychology, because of its causal and materialistic bias, has failed to lay hold of the tools which could do justice to the richness of the psyche. Wishing to preserve its identification with establishment science, it turned to behaviorism, a psychology without the psyche, which occupies itself with "the measurement of trivia."[28]

---

[27] *Mysterium Coniunctionis,* CW 14, par. 147.
[28] Christopher Lasch, *The Culture of Narcissism,* p. xiv.

Literature, too, which one might fondly imagine as a last bastion of the soul, has not neglected trivia. The distinguished literary critic and philosopher Henry Myers felt that scholars should

> devote a little less time to purely aesthetic and technical studies, to the elucidation of puzzling texts, and to literary history, and a little more time to the heart of literature—insight.[29]

By insight Myers means the ability to see things from within, for "the inner world of the human spirit is as boundless and wonderful as the outer world of the seven seas and the starry heavens."[30]

One could wish that poets, writers and critics might devote themselves to the service of that inner world which is so neglected in our time. Instead they have succumbed to the disjointed incrementalism endemic in our universities; in order to protect oneself against criticism and even ridicule the scholar must focus on fragments of the overall problem. Above all one must refrain from asking questions like, "What is this all about?"—perhaps because questions about meaning are often considered outside the scope of science.

And what would Jung say to contemporary "experts" who advise us to educate our children with more mathematics and engineering?

> It seems quite strange to me that one doesn't see what an education without the humanities is doing to man. He loses his connection with his family, as it were, with the whole stem, the tribe—the connection with the past that he lives in, in which man has always lived. Man has always lived in the myth, and we think we are able to be born today and to live in no myth, without history. That is a disease.[31]

Science, Religion and Psychotherapy

Jung calls our attention to the affinities between religion and therapy by pointing out that religion is our oldest psychotherapeutic system.

---

[29] "Literature, Science and Democracy," in W.R. Keast and R.E. Streeter, *The Province of Prose,* pp. 587-588.
[30] Ibid., p. 581.
[31] "The Houston Films," *C.G. Jung Speaking,* p. 348.

If you think of the various schools of psychotherapy as different religions it is easy to understand the hostility that has arisen among them.

For myself, it has been behaviorism (called by its adherents the most scientific of the psychologies) which has given the most offense. In its radical denial of the reality of the psyche and its mocking and contemptuous attitude toward those who believe in invisible forces, it has felt to me like a kind of sacrilege, a desecration of my highest values. But the day is coming soon when such arrogance will be checked and the soul's utterances will no longer be dismissed because unverifiable by modern science. What is it that verifies if not the psyches, the subjectivities, of men and women?

Jung also pointed out that religion stands on two legs, ritual and faith. These too are important ingredients in psychotherapy. The innovative psychoanalyst Robert Langs has shown how patients are exquisitely sensitive to deviations in the framework of psychotherapy. They unconsciously rely on the security provided by stable ground-rules (a set time, fee and physical setting, privacy and confidentiality, etc.). It is apparently through these rituals that the therapist communicates the ability to secure for the patient a free and protected space amidst the chaos and turmoil of everyday life. Psychotherapy partakes as well in faith inasmuch as both patient and therapist must trust that something constructive will emerge from "just talk."

Behaviorism and academic psychology concentrate on the animal nature of men and women to the exclusion of those qualities that make us human. They ignore the fact that we are in the process of participating in the birth of a new sensibility, as modern spiritual leaders point out. A new kind of spiritual being is about to be born and this consciousness will be as much of a quantum leap and as qualitatively different from the old consciousness as the latter was superior to animal consciousness.

It is true that in some ways we resemble the rat. And to forget our animal nature is to expose ourselves to a dangerous inflation. But the truth that we are like animals must be balanced with the equally weighty truth that we are also like gods. To forget our god nature is to risk a dangerous loss of self-esteem—a loss that is imperilling our civilization.

In the Old Testament the census is treated as if it were a dangerous, even evil, enterprise. Census-taking, that is, counting, can be understood psychologically as quantitative consciousness which in turn is equivalent to science.[32] If it is the primordial psyche, the unconscious, which speaks to us through Biblical imagery, then science (symbolized by the census), insofar as it emphasizes quantitative consciousness, may be an especially dangerous enterprise when applied to human beings.

Science treats not individuals but groups. Yet the defining characteristic of the human being is uniqueness, that which cannot be categorized. It is precisely those characteristics which do not qualify one for membership in any group or class whatsoever that define the individual. Or, as Jung said, "As the apotheosis of individuality, the self has the attributes of uniqueness and of occurring once only in time."[33]

The first symptoms of the coming rebellion against statistics are the enraged outcries of minority groups against being stereotyped. For instance, an individual woman rightly resists being characterized according to her membership in the group "women" and having traits assigned her which, while possibly true of women in general, may not apply to her. Most sympathize with her protest. We have grown so accustomed to the insistence on the particularity of the individual that we no longer recognize how extraordinary and how unprecedented in history it is.

What is being said here is not merely that each person is unique. As the word itself suggests, the "in-dividual" is not divided. One's uniqueness is the center, the cornerstone, the foundation upon which one's life rests. Uniqueness is the fount of life's struggles, or, to put it another way, in order for an individual to flourish, to realize one's

---

[32] See Edward F. Edinger, *The Bible and the Psyche: Individuation Symbolism in the Old Testament,* p. 90.

[33] *Aion,* CW 9ii, par. 115.

capacity as a human being, individuality must be borne its full term in the suffering of one's life. This process, called individuation, is to be distinguished from individualism, which is an egocentric attempt to set oneself apart from the mass.

Individuation means becoming special or bringing to fulfillment that which in oneself is unique. (To describe a human being as "unique" is in fact a redundancy.) What is brought forth is not necessarily exalted, nor even superior, merely singular.

It is the task of the individual to bring to birth that new existence, unanticipated and unprecedented in history, that has as its mission to testify to the sweetness and the majesty and the glory of God. In Jung's words, "The responsible living and fulfilling of the divine will in us will be our form of worship of and commerce with God."[34] Or as Clement of Alexandria put it, "When a man knows himself, he knows God."[35]

It could be said that in becoming what we were meant to become, we reveal the glory of God. No one knows, of course, what we were meant to be; our lives are the answer to that question and according to that answer God is justified or not; his plan is affirmed or not. Jung writes of individuation,

> Indeed, it seems as if all the personal entanglements and dramatic changes of fortune that go to make up the intensity of life were nothing but hesitations, timid shirkings, almost like petty complications and meticulous excuses manufactured to avoid facing the finality of this strange or uncanny process of crystallization.[36]

A mechanistic view of life has made this planet psychologically inhospitable to humans. We must not, cannot, will not abandon reason, logic and objectivity. But we must again assert the supremacy of the whole human being. The myth of the golem, the robot that takes over the world has already been realized. We are enslaved by the idea that we are simply machines. We have forgotten, as Jung

---

34 *Letters,* vol. 2, p. 316.
35 Quoted by Jung, *Aion,* CW 9ii, par. 347.
36 *Psychology and Alchemy,* CW 12, par. 326.

pointed out, that "man has a soul and there is a buried treasure in the field."[37] But, as he also said, man will not forever suffer his own nullification.

The era of science-as-religion departs; the era of science-as-tool approaches. We cannot continue to worship science because it is not broad enough to include all our capacities. It emphasizes the intellectual, thinking mode and omits feeling—that function which, near the end of his life, Jung said was "still largely lacking."[38] (The most original of our scientists, however, have included feeling. The late Nobel prize-winning physicist Paul Dirac wrote, "It is more important to have beauty in one's equations than to have them fit experiment.")

As the feminine principle symbolized by the Virgin Mary has now been enthroned in heaven (the Assumption of Mary), so also in the coming age will the feeling function, associated with the feminine principle, be recognized as equal in value to the thinking function.

---

[37] Quoted by Gerhard Adler, "Aspects of Jung's Personality and Work," p. 14.

[38] From the film *Matter of Heart*, quoted by Natalie S. Hayes, "Matter of Heart," p. 121.

8
Jewishness and Individuation

The Jew represents individuation.
—Edward F. Edinger, "Yahweh and Individuation."

How fair are your tents, O Jacob!
How fair your dwellings, Israel!
Like valleys that stretch afar,
like gardens by the banks of a river,
like aloes planted by Yahweh,
like cedars beside the waters!
A hero arises from their stock,
He reigns over countless peoples.
—Num. 24:5

A People Apart

See, a people dwelling apart, not reckoned among the nations.[1]

The Jews have always been a people without a country. Their allegiance has been to God, not to a nation-state. For a Jew to admit this may once have been shameful, even dangerous; but in our time all of us, if we are to survive, must have a primary allegiance to God and to the human spirit, never again to the nation-state.

The identity of the Jew, even in Biblical times not inextricably linked to locale, seems particularly well suited to modern times when, in Western lands, nationalism is on the wane. The Hebrews were nomads and sojourners in Egypt when we first encounter them in Genesis. Much of their glory, such as their receiving the Tablets of the Law from God, came to them while wandering in the desert.

---

[1] Num. 23:9, JB.

Location meant so little to the Father of the Jews, Abraham, that when with Lot he was looking for a place to settle he suggested, "Let there be no strife between you and me and between your herdsmen and my herdsmen. . . . Is not the whole land before you? . . . If you take the left hand, then I will go to the right; or if you take the right hand, then I will go to the left."[2] Lot chose for himself the lush Jordan Valley, but no matter, for the fact that the Lord was with Abraham rendered insignificant his choice of physical locale.[3]

In modern times the accession of the Jews to their own land, Israel, has only rendered more poignant the conflict between God and Caesar (for those who govern Israel are no less Caesar.) The laws that govern politics are of a different order from those that govern the inner world. As it is written, "You cannot serve God and mammon."[4]

Monotheism As Integrity

Hear O Israel: The Lord our God is one Lord.[5]

Jewish martyrs throughout the ages have died with these words, the *Shema,* on their lips—words which seem strangely inadequate to carry the weight of meaning they must once have carried. The central idea seemed to be that there was one God and the key lay in understanding the words on the subjective level, that is, as referring to the speaker's integrity. It made sense that one would be prepared to die rather than abandon his or her integrity. In psychological terms, the *Shema* was saying, "I am one. My integrity, intangible though it may be, is more important to me than my physical existence. My spirit is as real and valuable as my flesh." The Jews were the first to live this truth and whoever is truly a Jew lives it still.

---

2 Gen. 13:8-9, RSV.

3 A. Heschel, *The Sabbath,* pp. 3-10.

4 Matt. 6:24, Luke 16:13, RSV.

5 Deut. 6:4.

The reason Jews have contributed so much to world culture is perhaps their ability to maintain their integrity while being outcasts. This experience has given them access to the Self. They have been able to maintain their integrity because they have been buttressed with the belief that they are the chosen ones of God.

I once knew a young woman of little integrity. When some feeling or thought gave her more pain than she thought she could bear she would (not deliberately but instinctively, as it were) detach herself from that upsetting fact—repudiating it as if it were no longer a part of *her*. (Drug addicts also do this.) And in the end she, who sought to exclude something that belonged to her nature, found herself excluded. She became the outcast, the amputee, the unjustly abandoned one.

This process of detaching consciousness from an aspect of oneself is common enough, but in ethical terms it is illegitimate, in religious terms it is sinful and in psychiatric terms it is pathological. It leads, in ethical terms, to evil; in religious terms, to hell; and in psychological terms, to psychosis, drug addiction or criminality. Evil occurs when we lose touch with the source of the wound.[6]

To know that you are one, whole; to preserve your integrity at any cost—this is the psychological equivalent of monotheism and is identical with the attitude that the Jew proclaimed with his *Shema Yisrael*. It preserves us from evil and binds us to God, through all terror and turmoil, in an indissoluble bond. It also keeps us psychologically healthy. "Health," "whole," "holy," "heal"—do you see now why these words are connected etymologically? Because to be a person of integrity, to attain wholeness, also implies health and healing power which may be perceived as holiness.

There are patients who do not like their therapist to make connections between subjects. To some people their personality is like a collage composed of sectors which may or may not have anything to do with each other. Each sector or complex operates autonomously. This is psychological polytheism (in clinical terms, dissociation). For

---

6 See Myron B. Gubitz, "Amalek, The Eternal Adversary."

the monotheist everything is related to everything else, or rather, all things are related to one central thing, which is the one God. Another way to put it, perhaps, is that everything has a meaning. To the polytheist, to the pagan, meaninglessness is an acceptable, even desirable, condition. To the monotheist, to give up meaning would be like giving up God, the highest value. This must be why those Jewish martyrs died reciting the *Shema.* If a person has no integrity there can be no meaning, and vice versa, if one sees no meaning in life one can have no integrity.

The patients I've referred to are generally uncomfortable with the therapist relating their remarks to himself, the therapist. They insist that what they say should have no impact on the therapist, or at any rate, no emotional impact. Or rather, they want what they say to have no impact on the listener other than the one they choose.

In the outer world, too, we are advised not to take things personally. This is good advice if it is balanced with the ability to take seriously the feeling impact that events have on oneself. Otherwise we are left with an alienated modern "wasteland" man.[7]

The Vengefulness of Jews

C. S. Lewis confesses himself shocked by the maledictions so frequently encountered in the Psalms and he notes that while they are a "profoundly natural" reaction to injury, they are nonetheless "profoundly wrong."[8] As example he cites Psalm 109: "May his days be few, may his job be given to someone else. . . . When he is dead may his orphans be beggars."[9]

Another example is a familiar one: "Thou preparest a table before me in the presence of mine enemies."[10] I first encountered this innocuous-sounding line as a student in grammar school. (Our weekly

7 See T.S. Eliot, *The Complete Poems and Plays,* p. 21.
8 *Reflections on the Psalms,* p. 26.
9 Ibid., p. 20.
10 Ps. 23:5.

convocation would usually begin with a short scriptural reading.) The only way the line made sense to me was to understand that if I lived right, God might grant me such a relaxed attitude that I could enjoy a meal in front of my enemies. Without the intervention of God I was certain to suffer indigestion.

The Moffatt translation of the same line makes the meaning clearer. Psalm 23 reads, "Thou art my host spreading a feast for me while my enemies look on." Lewis observes, "The poet's enjoyment of his present prosperity would not be complete unless those horrid Joneses (who used to look down their noses at him) were watching it all and hating it."[11]

Lewis is inclined to excuse the vindictiveness of the Psalmists on the grounds that they were, after all, not Christians. But if they are to be excused on those grounds, he reasons, the pagan authors, being further removed from Christ, could be expected to curse and vilify their enemies still more than the Jews. Lewis's expectation is refuted by his examination of the pagan literature which yields not the "fury or luxury of hatred" found in the Psalms but "lasciviousness, much brutal insensitivity [and] cold cruelties taken for granted."[12] Thus Lewis is led reluctantly to the conclusion that "the Jews were much more vindictive and vitriolic than the Pagans."[13]

Lewis specifically refuses to take refuge in that "old gibe, 'How odd of God to choose the Jews,' "[14] but rather seeks a more substantive answer to the puzzling question of why the chosen people were possessed with vengefulness. He recalls a night spent on a train with a group of British soldiers during World War Two:

Their conversation made it clear that they totally disbelieved all that they had read in the papers about the wholesale cruelties of the Nazi regime. They took it for granted, without argument, that this was all lies, all propaganda put out by our own government to "pep up" our

---

11 *Reflections on the Psalms,* p. 21.

12 Ibid., p. 27.

13 Ibid., p. 28.

14 Ibid.

troops. And the shattering thing was that, believing this, they expressed not the slightest anger.[15]

To be convinced that their government was perpetrating a monstrous fraud upon them and *not* to react with anger seemed to Lewis to argue a "terrifying insensibility" which called into question their moral character, at least with regard to this issue. He concludes:

> If the Jews cursed more bitterly than the Pagans this was, I think, at least in part because they took right and wrong more seriously. . . . The Jews sinned in this matter worse than the Pagans not because they were further from God but because they were nearer to Him.[16]

Nearness to God, as Lewis recognized, is not an unalloyed blessing, for it can imbue one with God's wrath.

From the point of view of outer adaptation alone, however, the British soldiers were wise not to take things too seriously. In wartime, a worldly person expects lies and brutality from both sides.

The European, Jung often reminded us, is separated by only a few centuries from his barbarian ancestry over which the civilizing influence of Christianity forms but a thin veneer. The Jews, by contrast, were the first people (this, at any rate is the Judeo-Christian myth) to recognize the reality of a moral law which compensated for the selfish and brutal daily existence of our distant forebears. And with the Covenant the Jews contracted an enduring conscious and unconscious commitment to an inner moral order which (in accordance with the level of collective consciousness at the time) they conceived of as being handed down from Yahweh. Jews trace their ancestry to Adam whereas the "divinely stamped" portion of Gentile history goes back only to Christ.[17]

It would be strange indeed if this millennia-long disparity in experience between Jew and Christian were not somehow still operating.

---

[15] Ibid., p. 29.

[16] Ibid., pp. 30-31

[17] "Answer to Job," *Psychology and Religion,* CW 11, pars. 576-577, 618.

Jung and the Jews

Once during the early days of the Nazi regime Jung remarked that the Jewish psyche had less potential than that of the Christian. Partly because of its poor timing, this important observation was written off as anti-Semitism.

Anti-Semitism was endemic to the small-town Swiss culture of the late nineteenth century into which Jung was born and it would have been a miracle if he had not contracted a dose of it. All who knew him, however (and there were many Jews among his closest associates), have testified that with regard to individuals he never demonstrated the slightest prejudice.[18]

Jung called attention to the Jews' central contribution to Western culture. The idea of a "purposeful and morally inclined God" who took a special interest in mankind, he writes, "marked the end of the playful and rather purposeless existence of the polytheistic deities" of Greece and the Mediterranean.[19]

The Greeks' relationship to their gods (like the gods themselves) lacked feeling, while the Jewish relationship with God was more differentiated and more mutual. The Jews talked back to God, as in the incident where Abraham remonstrated with God over his wish to destroy Sodom and Gomorrah.[20]

Edinger, too, emphasizes the Olympians' lack of relationship with human beings. The Jews, by contrast, had

> a collective awareness of the numinous aspect of the psyche, i.e., Yahweh; and they related to it consistently in a mutual sense. The scriptures then represent the ongoing nature of that dialogue between God and man. That's unique . . . that experience has been the core of the Western psyche.[21]

---

18 Aniela Jaffé, "Jung and National Socialism," in *From the Life and Work of C.G. Jung,* offers a trenchant overview of Jung's supposed anti-Semitism.
19 *Letters,* vol. 2, p. 312.
20 Gen. 18:16-33.
21 "Yahweh and Individuation," public program, C.G. Jung Institute, San Francisco, 1974; see also *The Bible and the Psyche,* p. 12.

If Edinger's hypothesis is correct it would be equivalent to the Jews being the first born and the chosen and the sacrificed of God. That one fact, then, that the Jews were the first people to experience being personally called by God, can account for all of Jewish history including the persecutions. In the age that is now dawning, according to Jung and Edinger, God is seeking to incarnate in all of us.

When Jung said that the Jewish psyche (older and more developed, like the Chinese) had less potential than the Christian he had in mind something like electrical potential—that ego and unconscious were closer in the Jewish psyche (and hence there was less tension between them) than in the Christian. It is my experience, too, that the Jew tends to be on better terms with or more accepting of the shadow (one's more or less inferior side) than a Christian who often expects or aspires to be . . . well, more Christ-like. The greater distance between actuality and ideal creates a tension—like an electrical potential, which has a positive and a negative aspect. The positive aspect is the release of great quantities of energy which is conducive to new syntheses. The negative aspect is the greater likelihood of a split between conscious and unconscious, that is, dissociation.

Being a Jew

Behold a people.[22]

A young friend once asked me, "Why are so many psychologists Jews?" I answered, "Because we are 'a Kingdom of priests and a holy nation.' "[23] I explained that psychologists are the modern-day equivalent of priests in that they help people to orient themselves.

One could say, perhaps, that the Jews were a psychologically or religiously gifted people. Apparently, among all the nations, their psyches were the first to register a certain evolution of the God-image. From Hebrew festivals that originally celebrated the cycles of nature evolved festivals that celebrated events where God took an in-

---

[22] Num. 23:24, RSV.
[23] Exod. 19:6, RSV.

terest in the affairs of mankind. For instance, Passover, originally a spring festival, evolved into a commemoration of the flight from Egyptian slavery; the Feast of Weeks, a harvest festival, evolved into a commemoration of the handing down of the Torah to Moses at Mt. Sinai.[24] (And with the Christian dispensation, the Feast of Weeks further evolved into the descent of the Holy Spirit at Pentecost.)[25]

The idea is that what happens in the world means *me*. Carried to an extreme this would be schizophrenia. But the other extreme, to not take anything personally, deprives life of some of its meaning and results in an equally deadly condition, one which characterizes modern life. Because we cannot live this way we turn to drugs, war, sex —whatever makes us feel alive again, even if falsely.

Why are we Jews descended from Abraham, Isaac and Jacob? From Abraham because that old man never gave up, beginning over at age seventy, because he had so much faith in God; from Isaac because, as God's precious possessions, we are sacrificed; and from Jacob because God's favor was so important to us that (in collaboration with the conniving feminine) we stole our brother's birthright. And we carried our guilt with us into exile and did not shrink from wrestling with it when it appeared to us in the form of the Angel of God. We paid the price for our divine insolence with a permanent limp, but triumphed in the end.

Every Jewish family is literally an extended family—it extends back through the ages. We truly have Abraham, Isaac and Jacob as fathers—we are related to them through the spirit and through the blood. This gives us a sense of rootedness, meaning and continuity.

My twenty years of study of Jung's work have confirmed the truth of my first analyst's words to the effect that Jung puts people back in touch with their roots—Jews to Judaism, Christians to Christianity. At the same time, it makes the Jew aware of his or her inner Christian, while for the Christian it brings an awareness of the inner Jew.

---

24 See A. Heschel, *The Sabbath*, p. 7.
25 See also below, "Individuation and Pentecost."

When I began Jungian analysis I had not the least interest in either Judaism or Christianity. To be a Jew was at best an embarrassment and at worst an inexplicable and terrifying stigma. Unsuccessful in my attempts to understand it, pained and mortified, I tried to forget I was a Jew. Indeed, my experience contradicted the adage, "Let a Jew forget he's a Jew and a Christian will remind him of it in short order." In the circle of psychologically sophisticated Jews and Christians I traveled in, one could go for years between reminders.

There was no denying, though, that childhood experiences had marked me. I attempted to understand them by writing about them in the third person. For example:

A Street Encounter

The smiling, open intelligence of the little girl sitting proudly on her first tricycle, the bearded stranger approaching with a similar (surprising-in-an-adult) openness. He withholds acknowledgment of her friendliness, thinking, "Why should she feel so assured of a positive response? I, or even my children, could not have felt so confident. I could likely smile at a stranger and be greeted with, 'Are you a Jew? Spit in your shoe.' "

Even as a small child he knew of course that he was, alas, a Jew, but not wanting to spit in his shoe, nor to spit at all, nor have anyone spit at him, certainly, nor even to think of spit, he tried to reason with himself:

"What's so bad about spitting in my shoe?" (Shameful and unaccountably humiliating.)

He tried to reason away the unreasonably intense and persistent hurt.

"I wouldn't spit in my own shoe anyway—so it was only a harmless suggestion—not a reality." (Mortified, mortified.)

"It was so stupid." (Nothing helped.)

"What a mean man," thought the little girl.

As a child, to be a Jew marked one as weak, soft, vulnerable and, worst of all, feminine. This contrasted with what I aspired to be: strong, tough, masculine, powerful. I wanted to be a victor, not a victim. It boiled down to a pair of opposites, the bearded and bent old Jew and the erect, jack-booted Nazi. The Jew cowered and obeyed the shouted orders of the swaggering Nazi. Little inducement to be a Jew here. But what if I had been born in a small southern city, not a Jew?

The Serenity of a Small Southern Town:
An Unlived Life

Tennis rackets—that's one material object I know something about. They're cheaper ordered by mail. I ordered one for somebody's birthday. It didn't arrive on time so I called the mail-order house in North Carolina, long distance, angry.

I was connected with the assistant manager and my anger disappeared practically at the sound of his voice. He seemed bland, benign, well-intentioned and good. I felt him as well-meaning and myself as irrational. (He must have been somewhat in the wrong, though, because his explanation of how his clerk gave the wrong information was garbled.) All the clerks, with their soft southern drawls seemed kindly and well-disposed.

I wondered what it would be like to grow up in such an atmosphere. I imagined I would feel good and relaxed. That was another life that I hadn't lived—one maybe I could have lived, but hadn't.

Then I realized that Jews aren't allowed to live lives like that. The world that seems benign can turn persecutory at any moment, so a Jew must continue striving, his guard up. It would be idyllic to live in that southern town or any town where all is benign—but someone has to carry the shadow and the Jew is the chosen one.

A Jewish Boy

They hated me for no reason.[26]

A boy,[27] barely thirteen, small for his age (but self-possessed withal) absorbs the jibes and mockeries of his classmates. He says to them, in explanation of his laughing with them at a joke at his ex-

---

[26] John 15:25, Ps. 35:19, JB.
[27] Not the author.

pense, "I'm trying to go along with it." In response to their continued astonishment at his attitude he questions, "Do you need a reaction from me?" They deny this. They're cool. They don't *need* anything.

The boy enacts the role of the chosen one or of submission to a superior principle. For the other children he is the one who has not yet exchanged the glorious trappings of the original unconscious wholeness (the coat of many colors) for the new treasures of worldly status and prestige.

He is still true to himself; he has not abandoned his earliest dreams. The childhood self that his classmates think they wish to cast off they see reflected in him and naturally ridicule it. To them he must surely seem a "loser," one who has failed to make the transition from the now shameful glories of childhood to the more limited but more respectable goals of adulthood.

In a deeper sense he carries for them the image of Christ or of the Jew: soft, weak, devoted, sincere, receptive, true, pure, innocent of worldly ways. As it is written,

> If the world hates you, remember that it hated me before you. If you belonged to the world, the world would love you as its own; but because you do not belong to the world, because my choice withdrew you from the world, therefore the world hates you.[28]

The boy carries for his schoolmates the image of one still loyal to his inner nature and so is an object of derision for those who are becoming worldly wise. Because he is an introvert and of a religious disposition, he is more reluctant than they to exchange his original identification for one that is more socially acceptable. Of the primordial opposites, God and the world, he ever favors God. Thus he earns the enmity of men.

Of course his classmates are right; he must leave the Garden of Eden (and he knows this) but in casting his last loving glance homeward an image will be imprinted that he will carry with him into manhood, approach again perhaps in another form at mid-life and, if

---

[28] John 15:18-19, JB.

he has lived well, return to it at death. He will always maintain a connection to his original wholeness and this will make of him a religious man, a man of integrity, a Jew and a man for the new age. As T.S. Eliot wrote,

> We shall not cease from exploration
> And the end of all our exploring
> Will be to arrive where we started
> And know the place for the first time.[29]

Jews and Feeling

There is an obvious connection between Jews, the feeling function, the religious temperament, and the feminine principle. All are devalued in our culture.

But today, according to our culture's basic measure of value, money, it is not so much women who are disparaged, I think, as the feeling function. The traditionally masculine virtues of cool rationality and a disposition to organize and control are rewarded, while feeling values are belittled wherever they occur, in men or women.

The Nazis were great enemies of feeling, though friendly to inferior feeling, better known as sentimentality. (Goering, murderer of thousands, wept inconsolably when his pet canary died.) The Nazis made a sport of placing themselves in situations which would naturally elicit feeling, only to then deliberately withhold it. The one who exhibited the least feeling would be accounted the winner. We may fairly assume that Hitler himself unconsciously equated his inner feeling side, his shadow, with Jewishness, and experienced it as a threat to his masculine strength and purposiveness.

Thinking has given us science, with which indeed, as Jung notes, "one can open more doors than with bare hands."[30] And business,

---

[29] "Little Gidding," lines 239-242, in *The Complete Poems and Plays,* p. 145.

[30] "Commentary on *The Secret of the Golden Flower,*" *Alchemical Studies,* CW 13, par. 2.

too, proceeds primarily under the banner of Logos. Compared to this, what has feeling to offer?

Many (and this is characteristic of men and the masculine principle) have a thought and then assume that something has changed when in fact nothing has changed. One has to live one's truth in order for it to be realized. This takes time and requires a rare absolutism of conviction and thought which has a religious quality and is related to the feeling function.[31]

It never occurs to many men that only by living their thoughts and convictions do those thoughts become real. So thoroughly do they equate thoughts and reality that such a book as this is likely to be taken for an assemblage of words—some of them clever perhaps, but words nonetheless, which can be disputed by other words. The fact that these words, these thoughts, have been lived, have blood coursing through them, counts for little. To the "nothing-but" intellectual, it is all word play. This is because of an inferior feeling function which, when developed, gives life and body to thoughts.

Saturn is the planetary deity of the Jews. In alchemy it is associated with coagulation (incarnation), as well as with desirousness.[32] Coagulation is also associated with the feminine principle which makes things real, that is, incarnates invisible forces like ideas and thoughts. The idea of desirousness is important because it is through the encounter between instinctive desirousness and spirituality that psychic transformation takes place. In this the Jew has the advantage because Jews are usually more accepting of certain aspects of their instinctuality.

The Jews are a religious and a feeling people. The following retells one of Ginzberg's legends of the Jews.

> When God was looking for a people to adopt his Torah he first queried the Ammonites, asking, "Will you accept my Torah?"
> After thinking about it a while they replied, "What's in it?"

---

[31] See Jung, *Dream Analysis: Notes of the Seminar in 1928-1930,* p. 658.
[32] See Edinger, *Anatomy of the Psyche: Alchemical Symbolism in Psychotherapy,* pp. 86-90.

God answered, "Thou shalt not kill."

"Oh, that would be a problem for us since we are a warrior people," replied the Ammonites.

So God asked the Moabites, "Will you accept my Torah?"

After thinking about it for a while they replied, "What's in it?"

God answered, "Thou shalt not steal."

"Oh, we are a merchant people you see and a prohibition like that could endanger our livelihood," replied the Moabites.

So God asked the Israelites, "Will you accept my Torah?"

And the Israelites answered unhesitatingly, "Na-a-seh V'nishma," meaning, "Yes, and we'll think about it later."[33]

This is the way of the feeling function: devoted, loyal, sincere, wholehearted, capable of great courage and the love which is strong as death.[34]

Individuation and Sacrifice (Passover)

The killing of all of the Egyptian first-born children was the tenth, final and convincing plague that the Lord sent down against the stubbornly resisting Pharaoh. Only the most terrible affliction, apparently, could serve to bend his will.

Our ego is like Pharaoh and clings to old attitudes despite multiple misfortunes. Often only a stunning and decisive defeat has the power to effect a genuine reversal of attitude. On several occasions Pharaoh agreed to let the Israelites go but reneged the moment he was released from what was plaguing him. We too, when cast down by God, may vow to change, but upon deliverance from our current affliction soon lapse back into habitual, inauthentic ways of being which do not express our true, currently unfolding nature.

Edinger tells us that the Israelites represent an ego that is in touch with the Self (God).[35] According to the Passover myth this ego will

---

[33] See Louis Ginzberg, *Legends of the Jews,* vol. 3, p. 81.

[34] Song of Sol. 8:6.

[35] *The Bible and the Psyche: Individuation Symbolism in the Old Testament,* p. 12.

be spared the death of its highest value (the first born) but only on condition of a sacrifice. Scripture designates an animal sacrifice, a lamb "without blemish," the blood of which was to be daubed on the lintel and door posts (the sacred places) of each Israelite home as a sign to the Avenging Angel of the Lord to pass over that house which had a relationship to God.[36]

The myth tells us that there must be a sacrifice of an unblemished lamb in order to make it possible for the new Self to live. But what does the lamb symbolize? In early Christian times it came to symbolize Christ. Therefore the blood of the lamb alludes to the blood of Christ which has power to redeem.

The lamb may also represent that childishness that keeps us from taking hold in this world; that is, by harking back to the childish, paradisiacal world, our "lambishness" keeps us from accepting our current world as fully real. We unconsciously live the "provisional life,"[37] which prevents us from being transformed by our contact with reality and from having an effect on the world. This complex of childishness must be dissolved and its libido released so as to infuse the new Self with creative energy. In religious language, "The blood of Christ . . . can purify our inner self from dead actions so that we do our service to the living God."[38]

Hence the lamb without blemish can symbolize an attitude which has outgrown its usefulness (a neurosis, for instance) and needs to be sacrificed and replaced with an attitude that better fits the present circumstances. And this not just in order to produce a better outward adaptation, but in order to complete God's work through our act of recognizing (not grudgingly and not just intellectually) that this wonderful world that He created really exists.

Just as man needs God so also God needs man, that He may be realized and live in this world. Jung wrote:

---

[36] Exod. 12.

[37] See Daryl Sharp, *The Survival Papers: Anatomy of a Midlife Crisis,* pp. 87-88.

[38] Heb. 9:14, JB.

From a low hill in the Athi plains of East Africa I once watched the vast herds of wild animals grazing in soundless stillness, as they had done from time immemorial, touched only by the breath of a primeval world. I felt then as if I were the first man, the first creature, to know that all this *is*. The entire world round me was still in its primeval state; it did not know that it *was*. And then, in that one moment in which I came to know, the world sprang into being; without that moment it would never have been. All Nature seeks this goal and finds it fulfilled in man, but only in the most highly developed and most fully conscious man. Every advance, even the smallest, along this path of conscious realization adds that much to the world.[39]

Just as a child cannot truly recognize its parents until it has developed an independent standpoint which allows for some emotional and psychological distance from them, so we cannot fully appreciate the world until we have "put away childish things." A too-innocent, unrealistically pure and trusting childishness (in dreams and myths often symbolized by children) must be sacrificed. The killing of children in myth or dream, writes Edinger, may be interpreted as "the *mortificatio* of infantile desirousness and the extraction of libido from immature modes of being."[40] It can help free us from childish habits to know that we are sacrificing them to a higher purpose. Thus, as Jung points out,

"For those who have a symbol, the passing from one side to the other, the transmutation, is easier." In other words, those who have no symbol will find it very difficult to make the transition.[41]

Abraham, like God, loved so much that he was willing to sacrifice his first-born son (his highest value). The first born is consecrated to

---

[39] "Psychological Aspects of the Mother Archetype," *The Archetypes and the Collective Unconscious,* CW 9i, par. 177.

[40] "The Christian Archetype," public program, C.G. Jung Institute, San Francisco, 1980; see also *The Anatomy of the Psyche,* pp. 147ff, *The Bible and the Psyche,* p. 51, and *The Christian Archetype,* p. 91.

[41] *Nietzsche's Zarathustra: Notes of the Seminar Given in 1934-1939,* vol. 2, p. 1248. The sentence quoted is, writes Jung, "in the 16th-century Latin text of one of my old Hermetic philosophers."

God but can be redeemed by the sacrifice of a lamb. (In Abraham's case it was perhaps his rash impulsivity, his "ram-nature," which had to undergo transformation, since it was finally the ram which was sacrificed.)[42]

In our era the sacrifice of Christ will be superseded by the conscious and repeated (though usually unwilling) sacrifice of the individual's highest ego value. The following is an example from my personal experience. While waiting for a red light to change I realized that even being caught by a red light registered on my consciousness as a defeat. Then I thought of my "Passover" dream, which read in part as follows:

> I am witnessing a dramatic performance in which the audience participates by suggesting lines of development. I am watching the terrible mortification of this woman. Everything turned out exactly as she would not have wanted it. She is transfigured, purified and dying. Then other women are dying though some are happy.
> I ask, "Why are some of you happy?"
> "Because we refrain from self-punishment."
> I don't know how to resolve the action dramatically, so it lags. I dismiss as banal (in true introvert's fashion) a young extravert's suggestion that you can't distinguish human blood from neutral (animal) blood.

Months later it occurred to me that the neutral blood might stand for the ability to conceptualize or symbolize. I asked myself why God was content with the blood of the lamb in place of the first born. Why did he accept the "neutral" blood (in relation to which our feelings or emotions are not so activated) in place of the real thing?

I realized that nothing compelled me to sacrifice my blood, my real life; my fantasy or symbolic life would do. That is, for someone like myself, whose impulse is to become fully immersed in the here-and-now, it has been hard to learn that the world of the intellect and of the imagination is real and valid. I wondered if I had been overly impressed with the Old Testament prohibition against graven images.

---

[42] See *The Bible and the Psyche*, pp. 32-35, and *The Creation of Consciousness: Jung's Myth for Modern Man*, p. 97.

Then I reminded myself that in the Old Testament itself there is at least one allusion to the healing power of image-making. In Numbers 21 it is recorded how the Israelites, impatient of their wanderings in the desert, spoke against God and Moses. Then God sent down fiery serpents whose bite brought death. When Moses interceded for the people, God told him to fashion a bronze serpent which when contemplated by the victim provoked recovery.

In the same way, if we can make a representation of what has "bitten" us by drawing, painting, clay modeling, conceptualizing, writing, dramatizing or portraying it through movement or dance, that process can help us separate ourselves from the unconscious complex that has poisoned us, thereby promoting healing by promoting consciousness (differentiation).

Sacrifice can be understood psychologically as the giving over of life energy for the purposes of the inner world, for instance by paying attention to dreams and the whisperings of the soul, which often expresses itself in complaints, resentments and unrealistic longings, all of which our ego (Pharaoh) is apt to dismiss as unworthy.

By taking these things seriously, however, we may avert plagues falling upon our head. Whatever is not brought into consciousness may have to be lived as fate.

Individuation and the Holy Spirit (Pentecost)

In Acts we read:

> When the day of Pentecost had come, they were all together in one place. And suddenly a sound came from heaven like the rush of a mighty wind, and it filled all the house where they were sitting. And there appeared to them tongues as of fire, distributed and resting on each one of them. And they were filled with the Holy Spirit and began to speak in other tongues, as the Spirit gave them utterance.[43]

The scriptural narrative goes on to describe how a crowd, many of whom were foreigners, quickly gathered, and how each listener (this

---

[43] Acts 2:1-4, RSV.

was the wonder of it) heard the apostles speaking in his or her own tongue.

This story reminded me of an experience recounted by Gerhard Adler—how upon departing from a lecture of Jung's he shared with friends his astonishment that in his talk Jung seemed to be addressing Adler's precise concerns. To Adler's surprise both his friends took exception, each claiming that *their* own personal, quite different pre-occupations were what Jung had been addressing.[44]

I have heard and read similar accounts from other patients of Jung's in which he seemed to be speaking to the very essence of their concerns—concerns which they had not yet revealed to him. For instance, there are accounts of patients coming to their session prepared to discuss an important dream but treated instead to an hour-long monologue from Jung. The amazing thing was that Jung's words seemed in the highest degree relevant to their dream and they departed feeling that no direct interpretation could have achieved more for their understanding of it. This seems to be what happens in the company of one who is speaking from the Self, that is, out of a connection with God or out of his or her wholeness.

In the scriptural passage we are considering, Peter quotes the words of the prophet Joel in explanation of the phenomenon of speaking in tongues:

And in the last days it shall be, God declares, that I will pour out my Spirit upon all flesh, and your sons and your daughters shall proph-esy, and your young men shall see visions, and your old men shall dream dreams.[45]

The idea is that in the age we are now entering, the age of the indwelling of the Holy Spirit, every man and woman will be capable of gaining access to the depths out of which Jung spoke. It is when we can leave our personal complexes behind that our experience at-tains more universal relevance. This cannot be achieved through an

---

44 "Aspects of Jung's Personality and Work," p. 11.
45 Acts 2:17, RSV.

egocentric wish for power, but is a grace bestowed upon one. As Jesus said, "You did not choose me, no, I chose you."[46]

Individuation and the Jews

I try to make the distinction which Jung made between the inner and outer world, the subjective and the objective. I try to show how one compensates for the other (as dreams conpenwate for our conscious attitude), and how one is as valuable as the other. For me being chosen by God (psychologically: hearing the call to individuation) is every bit as valid as "honor, power, wealth, fame and the love of women[47]—that is, worldly success. To reduce this need of the soul to a mother or father complex represents the Freudian, worldly view, which is precisely what Jung's work compensates for. Not that it is wrong, but it is only half right and therefore in need of something to balance it. By itself it is deadly to the spirit.

Being chosen (as the Jews were) entails an acceptance of one's destiny to serve as a vessel for God's transformation in us through the work of the Holy Spirit. But the path of individuation can be a lonely one. Here is an old story that illustrates the point:

> Two Jews are taking a walk. Two roughnecks are walking behind them, mocking them.
> "Do we have to take this?" asks one of the Jews.
> The other replies, "What's the matter with you? They are together and we are alone."

The implication here is that because the usual outer, collective paths to power were less accessible to the Jew—in the past more than now—he was granted access to the inner path of individuation (in accordance with the psychological law of compensation whereby defeats in the outer world are balanced by opportunity in the inner world).

---

[46] John 15:16, JB.

[47] Sigmund Freud, "Introductory Lectures on Psychoanalysis," *Standard Edition of the Complete Psychological Works,* vol. 16, p. 376.

Let the following serve as a contribution toward an understanding of what it means that the Jews are a "chosen people."

First, they did not seek to be chosen.

Second, even if being chosen were desired it could not be achieved by means of a conscious decision.

Third, being chosen is paid for with a terrible price, as the history of the Jews or the life of Christ readily shows. As it is written, "They hated me for no reason."[48]

Fourth, as we enter now into the age of the Holy Spirit, all of us, as chosen ones, will be called upon to suffer the fate of the Jewish people and of Christ. As Jung writes:

Insofar as the archetypal content of the Christian drama was able to give satisfying expression to the uneasy and clamorous unconscious of the many, the *consensus omnium* raised this drama to a universally binding truth—not of course by an act of judgment, but by the irrational fact of possession, which is far more effective. Thus Jesus became the tutelary image or amulet against the archetypal powers that threatened to possess everyone. The glad tidings announced: "It has happened, but it will not happen to you inasmuch as you believe in Jesus Christ, the Son of God!" Yet it could and it can and it will happen to everyone in whom the Christian dominant has decayed. For this reason there have always been people who, not satisfied with the dominants of conscious life, set forth—under cover and by devious paths, to their destruction or salvation—to seek direct experience of the eternal roots, and, following the lure of the restless unconscious psyche, find themselves in the wilderness where, like Jesus, they come up against the son of darkness.[49]

To my Jewish brethren: Here is a solution to "the Jewish Question." Accept that you, as one marked of God, a chosen one, are fated to be persecuted. A hard fate, you say? True, but there are compensations for being God's elect.

It is clear to me that many of the traits of Jews, positive and negative, can be traced to their chosenness. Why have they been preemi-

---

[48] John 15:25, Ps. 35:19, JB.
[49] *Psychology and Alchemy,* CW 12, par. 41.

nent in multiple fields of endeavor? Because they are subject to a dynamism that says, "You are the heir of God's kingdom." Great expectations can lead to great deeds as well as to folly.

Or to answer in another way the same question, "Why have the Jews achieved so much?" Because of the Covenant, the life of the individual, solitary, restless Jew is important to God. In the coming age of the indwelling of the Holy Spirit (the Psychological dispensation), this Covenant is being extended to all of humanity. We Jews will soon be relieved of the burden we have carried these four thousand years. We are now being joined by our non-Jewish sisters and brothers who are rapidly becoming conscious of their call into God's service as chosen ones.

Why We Must Remember the Holocaust

I can only glimpse the Holocaust out of the corner of my eye, so to speak, or in those unguarded moments when it unexpectedly looms into consciousness. If I try to focus on it, it immediately begins to expand explosively, like a star in its birth throes, so that it soon exceeds by far my powers of comprehension.

Perhaps we can look at the holocaust as a collective sacrifice—of God's eldest son, the Jewish people. As the sacrifice of Christ initiated the Piscean age, so the sacrifice of the Jews foreshadows the Aquarian age. In return for this sacrifice, in accordance with the law of compensation, we may expect some manifestation of God's grace. But because this event is still so incomprehensible to human consciousness we must find a way to keep its memory before us. This is the reason for memorializing the holocaust—because we do not yet understand it.

9

The Sabbath, God's Only Daughter

Busy, busy, busy.
—Popular saying.

Nobody has time anymore to look at a flower.
—Georgia O'Keefe.

The Jews' Great Contribution

If, as I once read in a statistics book of all places, "The world of reality is a world of limitations,"[1] the inner world would be, by contrast,
a world of absolutes. We need absolutes to live fully. For instance,
we need to know that in a certain sense each one of us is of infinite
value.

The Israelites were the first to worship a God who loved them to
excess. To God they were special, a holy people that He bound to
Himself in a covenant. Jung writes,

[Yahweh] compelled a personal relationship between himself and
man, who could not help but feel personally called by him. That was
the essential difference between Yahweh and the all-ruling Father
Zeus, who in a benevolent and somewhat detached manner allowed
the economy of the universe to roll along on its accustomed courses
and punished only those who were disorderly. He did not moralize
but ruled purely instinctively. He did not demand anything more
from human beings than the sacrifices due to him; he did not want to
do anything *with* human beings because he had no plans for them.
Father Zeus is certainly a figure but not a personality. Yahweh, on
the other hand, was interested in man. Human beings were a matter
of first-rate importance to him. He needed them as they needed him,
urgently and personally. . . . Against mankind as a whole [Zeus] had

---

[1] Q. McNemar, *Psychological Statistics.*

123

no objections—but then they did not interest him all that much. Yahweh, however, could get inordinately excited about man as a species and men as individuals if they did not behave as he desired or expected.[2]

Interpreted psychologically, bondage to God in a covenant suggests that in order to keep one's integrity one must regularly turn one's attention inward (toward God). This is why keeping the Sabbath day holy is one of the Ten Commandments. It means the same as turning one's energies inward, away from worldly concerns, a sacrifice because it produces no tangible result. The world, on the other hand, would claim *all* of our energies. The list of important things to do in the world is endless.

The Sabbath as Release from This World

The eleventh chapter of Matthew opens with what could be construed as Jesus evaluating the "success" of his ministry. First John the Baptist questions Jesus' authority. Then Jesus berates his contemporaries for their resistance to the Gospel. Next in the scriptural narrative Christ appears to rediscover his proper connection to the Self (God) with the words, "Yea, Father, for such was thy gracious will."[3] Then, having recovered his equilibrium, he preaches a relationship to the Self in which the ego is humble and submissive, not inflated with power drives and lust for gain from which even Jesus, partaking of our human nature, was not immune. He invites us,

> Come to me, all who labor and are heavy-laden, and I will give you rest. Take my yoke upon you, and learn from me; for I am gentle and lowly in heart, and you will find rest for your souls. For my yoke is easy, and my burden is light.[4]

In our day, no less than in Jesus', many are laden with worry, toil and care. We may consider this state to be no more than the fulfill-

---

2 "Answer to Job," *Psychology and Religion,* CW 11, par. 568.
3 Matt. 11:26, RSV.
4 Matt. 11:28-30, RSV.

ment of our obligation to the outer world, but from the point of view of the inner world, all that outwardly directed work may not be necessary. Work can and will take up all of one's time and energy with nothing left over for God. The subjective world, the psyche, the eternal world, will be neglected. That is why the Sabbath was created—to demarcate and structure a regular and collectively sanctioned time when individuals could be freed from worldly obligations.

The demands made upon us by the physical universe are infinite. To cite just one example, the possibilities of home improvement are limitless. Cooking and cleaning and washing and shopping and gardening and child-care and car-care and care of clothing and record-keeping and errand-running—the list is endless. That is why we need the Sabbath—so we can devote ourselves to the inner world.

That these speculations are not lacking foundation is suggested by the sequence of events in the gospels, where, in the very next episode, the subject of the Sabbath comes up. Jesus and his disciples are challenged as to their actions on the Sabbath and Jesus declares, "The Sabbath was made for man, and not man for the Sabbath."[5] (This is in accord with the new dispensation which supersedes the Law; the Word of God is no longer writ indelibly in stone but is revealed in dialogue with man.)

Prayer: Restore to Us the Holy Sabbath, O Lord

Do you know what this could mean? Can you imagine a day reserved each week when work (even that which is pleasing to some, like gardening or home improvement) would be forbidden?

We would have no choice but to prune our souls, repair our minds and order our relationships with our loved (and hated) ones again. The TV and the stereo would be silenced, likewise the intrusive ring of the devil's own device, the telephone; so too would that aggressive machine, the auto, be stilled.

---

5 Mark 2:27, RSV.

Perusing that silent sea of time, what unsuspected thoughts or feelings might arise. One could just stay home and talk. Talk to another or to oneself. Commune with oneself. Talk and listen. Can you imagine the stillness, the silence?

Silent the motorcycles, the lawnmowers and the leaf-blowers, the buzz of the chain saws, too. A kind of Christmas once a week, a night, holy and still, and a day, holy and still. Can you imagine, in that silence, what healing? Restore to us the Holy Sabbath, O Lord.

How the Sabbath Imposed Itself on Me

I have had as much trouble as the next person in setting aside a Sabbath. But I noticed that on Friday night an atmosphere of tension frequently prevailed in our home, as if my whole family were expecting something—"satisfaction of our needs" is the way I put it to myself. It was as if we had worked hard all week and expected a reward. (Perhaps that cycle of work and reward, written in our bones, reflects the archetype of the Sabbath.)

As the children grew older and more differentiated, it became harder to agree on what kind of food to have or what movie to see or for that matter whether to go out at all. So family members more and more pursued their satisfactions individually.

Perhaps the precious and fulfilling reward for a week's work would have been the reuniting of the family in wholeness and harmony, as if all the contending fragments had at last been reconciled. The paradisal feeling that accompanies this fantasy is an expression of the family archetype in its positive aspect.

But only something of higher value than any individual ego can provide a center capable of drawing all the diverse egos together. On the Sabbath, "in the midst of silence," we once contemplated God. But we are now, for a short time in history, orphaned from God, and because we lack a center (something more important than ego concerns) our children too are orphaned.

Then for many years, when I tried to work late on Friday or on Saturday, a kind of toxic fatigue would come over me. I kept right on working, hardly noticing it, but over the years it grew more marked. And a few years later when I had demanding parental responsibilities on top of a full-time practice and desperately sought to find time for writing, I found myself suffering from a more potent version of that toxic exhaustion syndrome which made it impossible to work past a certain hour. Usually the fatigue hit me late Friday afternoon, although it was also dependent on how hard I had worked that week, particularly that day. If the rest of the week had been easy I might be able to work late on Friday.

Then Saturday: I was usually able to work quite well Saturday morning but only for a couple of hours—then that overpowering fatigue bid me shut down my computer. Mid or late afternoon on Saturday (depending on how hard I had worked that weekend) I would then typically begin to feel a release of that tension and be capable of working again.

The approximation, with increasing age and decreasing energy, of my inner cycle to the Jewish Sabbath was quite apparent. It made me wonder and still does. I still cannot bring myself to take off a whole twenty-four hours for God's sake. I have various reasons that I give myself. Meanwhile I continue to watch the cycle impose itself upon me.

I now recognize it is not merely reward that the Sabbath is about but death and rebirth. Death, because letting go of the work week means acceptance of the defeats and disappointments that were inherent in it—admitting I didn't accomplish as much as I had hoped. Rebirth, because in that process my sins, mostly shortcomings, are forgiven (or, increasingly with age, forgotten) and I am cleansed and prepared to approach the world afresh. And writing this I realize some people must accomplish the same thing with leaf-blower or dirt bike (but must it *blast* so?)

What the Sabbath Does for Us

It is a symptom of our spiritually benighted age that the impact the Sabbath day could have on our lives has been forgotten. As the shadows lengthen on a Friday eve, a gentle hush falls upon the *shtetl* and the holy Sabbath, as a bride, prepares to make her entrance. Then the cares of this world are dispelled and a beautiful silence remains to greet her. As Jesus said, "In the world you will have tribulation; but be of good cheer, I have overcome the world."[6]

There is no end of troubles in the world, for its limitations are inescapable. The maladjusted person is one who refuses to admit the relativity, complexity and impersonality of the outer world and imposes upon it the inner world of absolutes in an illegitimate (that is, unadapted) fashion.

The world of reality is a world in which everything is relative, everything is conditional. It is a realm of parts. There is always another side to be considered, and the issues are usually complex and multifaceted, denying us the satisfaction of a simple solution. The Sabbath is meant to compensate for this "gray world with its boxes"[7] by giving us an experience of eternity, a timeless, limitless world. "The Sabbath is God's only daughter."[8]

Something Within Can Redeem Us

My kingdom is not of this world.[9]

> The kingdom of heaven is like a treasure hidden in a field which someone has found; he hides it again, goes off happy, sells everything he owns and buys the field.[10]

Jung's commentary on these lines is worth quoting at length:

> The aim of the great religions is expressed in the injunction "not of this world," and this implies the inward movement of libido into the unconscious. Its withdrawal and introversion create in the uncon-

---

[6] John 16:33, RSV.

[7] Jung, *Memories, Dreams, Reflections,* p. 295.

[8] A.J. Heschel, *The Sabbath.*

[9] John 18:36.

[10] Matt. 13:44, JB.

scious a concentration of libido which is symbolized as the "treasure." . . .

. . . The soul is a personification of the unconscious, where lies the treasure, the libido which is immersed in introversion and is allegorized as God's kingdom. This amounts to a permanent union with God, a living in his kingdom, in that state where a preponderance of libido lies in the unconscious and determines conscious life. The libido concentrated in the unconscious was formerly invested in objects, and this made the world seem all-powerful. God was then "outside," but now he works from within, as the hidden treasure conceived as God's kingdom.[11]

Jung's message may be summarized in the words, "Man has a soul and there is a treasure buried in the field." The field is an individual's subjective experience. In our time it is thought to be of little value. The treasure is God, the highest value. Another way to say it is that if we live our life true to our inner experience, fully, sincerely and devotedly (as Jesus did), we will find redemption; psychologically speaking, we will be more complete, that is, individuated.

Everything we need is to be found within us. This is a truth that is hard to hold onto partly because in the world's most extraverted society, America, we are constantly being assured that what we need lies outside of us, in the shopping center, the church social hall or the university.

And the pundits scratch their heads wondering, "Why, when Americans are better off economically than they've ever been before, is the national mood so discontented?" No better answer exists than may be found in scripture, "Man shall not live by bread alone, but by every word that proceeds from the mouth of God."[12] Or as Jung reminded us, we have "forgotten why man's life should be sacrificial."[13]

---

[11] *Psychological Types,* CW 6, pars. 423-424.

[12] Matt. 4:4, Deut. 8:3, RSV.

[13] "Psychology and Religion," *Psychology and Religion,* CW 11, par. 133.

Psychotherapy as Sabbath

For some the weekly psychotherapy hour now serves as a kind of Sabbath. At that appointed day and time the patient's thoughts turn inward as he or she pauses and asks, "Who am I that all this should have happened to me?" This question reflects the religious attitude, which considers carefully one's experience and takes the subject of the experience (oneself) into full account.

As a psychotherapist I feel I perform no more important function than to hold the psychotherapeutic hour sacred, thereby affirming the dignity and the worth of the inner world. I have it as a rule that unless I receive twenty-four hours' notice, patients are charged for the hour whether or not they make use of it. The apparent harshness of the rule is to help keep the psychotherapeutic hour inviolable. The demands of the inner world are easily set aside because the unconscious speaks at first in whispers. The penalty for violating the Sabbath in Biblical times was death. The penalty was severe not only because of the weight given that commandment by our fathers but because of the ease with which worldly matters take precedence over matters of the soul.

Cancellations are infrequent in my practice but this week I had two. I spoke to both patients briefly on the phone. The young man said that his long-awaited motorcycle was ready and he was anxious to pick it up. The young woman explained she had to take her mother to the hospital and besides she had to work. For both patients it was their first cancellation. When I next see them I will bring up the subject. And in discussing it I think they will realize that there is at least one person in the world, their therapist, who believes that what goes on inside of them, their psyche, is as important as their outer affairs.

I find I influence my patients to take their inner world more seriously because I take it seriously—not only in my words but in my life. So when I have such a rule as this, and when in addition I start my sessions on time and finish on time, my actions bear witness to my belief in the sanctity of the psychotherapeutic hour.

Some of my fellow therapists think that it expresses a healthy liberality of mind to, say, extend the psychotherapy hour when the patient is late, or to make last-minute changes in scheduling to accommodate patient or therapist. But the message that comes across unconsciously, I think, is that the therapy hour must give way to worldly considerations, that is, Caesar's world is more important than God's.

And when patients consider cutting down the frequency of their appointments or terminating altogether, therapists are often loath to oppose their will, thinking they have no right to try to keep the patient in therapy. There are times, however, when patients need encouragement to set aside a regular time to attend to that depreciated and neglected part of themselves, the "least of these my brethren," that is so deserving of respect and consideration.

By contrast the extraverted attitude is focused on the goal, an attitude which, while perfectly appropriate in its own domain, is not appropriate to the inner world where activities characterizing the feminine spirit predominate: circumambulating, accepting, waiting, ripening. Let us not emulate the ancient Romans who, when they first encountered the Hebrews, ascribed their observance of a day of rest to indolence.[14] It reflects not indolence but a consciousness which recognizes the existence and importance of an inner world. And as in the outer world, attention and devotion to the inner is likely to be rewarded, one such reward being enhanced self-esteem. In fact the conviction, rooted in the blood, that "God cares what I do with my life," may account for the preeminence of Jews in so many fields of endeavor.

In this dark age of the soul, the West has forgotten how to look at things with the inner eye. Not only has Jung called this one-sidedness to our attention (others have done the same) but he has revisioned the subjective aspect of life (for that is what we are missing) in psychological terms which are more acceptable to our reason. As it is written:

---

14 A.J. Heschel, *The Sabbath*, p. 13.

For this commandment which I command thee this day, it is not hidden from thee, neither is it far off. It is not in heaven. . . . Neither is it beyond the sea. . . . But the word is very nigh unto thee, in thy mouth, and in thy heart, that thou mayest do it.[15]

In other words, observance of the Sabbath, or engagement in an equivalent activity such as psychotherapy which honors the inner world, may provide us with access to it. Therefore, as it is written, "Choose life, that both thou and thy seed may live."[16]

---

[15] Deut. 30:11-14.
[16] Deut. 30:19.

10
The Feminine in the Godhead

Let the light that I have carried in my womb shine forth.
—Inscription on a stone carving by C.G. Jung.

That which is conceived in her is of the Holy Spirit.
—Matt. 1:20, RSV.

Prologue

Women increasingly outnumber men (by two to one or more) as students of psychotherapy, patients in psychotherapy and consumers of psychological goods (lectures, conferences, books). Expecting my readers, too, would be mainly women, I have felt myself to be speaking to them throughout the writing of this book.

Why then the necessity for a separate chapter on the feminine? This is a question I asked myself unceasingly as I labored over this chapter that didn't want to be written. From the inception of this book I had meant to reserve a special place for the feminine. I collected ample notes but only a few coherent pages could I create from all my research. I concluded that the feminine desires embodiment and slips through word nets no matter how cunningly conceived. I have come to believe that it reigns over a realm of silence, or, as in a woman's dream, a humming.[1] Fear of being perceived as stereotyping women added to my difficulty. Apparently the feminine, as I experience it, doesn't want to be written about; but then again, maybe it does.

This book is an experiential work in the sense that everything in it I have experienced from the inside. Of the feminine too, I have per-

---

[1] Elaine Stanton, personal communication.

sonal experience, but as a man. I have not identified with the feminine side of my nature. I see women through male eyes. This makes my viewpoint limited and biased. I admit that limitation and that bias.

Nothing in life has moved me so much as bearing witness in the lives of patients, friends and others, to the mysterious unfolding of a unique human personality, one which had always been present but hidden. In the words of the Lord to the prophet, "Before I formed you in the womb I knew you, and before you were born I consecrated you."[2] The individuation of women as well as men is what touches me most deeply. Anything in this book, if it hampers that process, has missed its mark. I am aware that modern women, conditioned by centuries of masculine "understanding" of their nature must sometimes protect themselves from it. My generalizations are meant to describe a principle in nature, not to apply to the case of an individual woman who may or may not participate in that particular aspect of the feminine principle.

While I attempt to distinguish between the feminine principle and actual women, women instinctively feel the projection of my feminine nature upon them. This, too, may annoy them. Moreover, the projections are directed at them in the form of words, concepts and judgments. Many women retain a particular susceptibility to them because the Logos side of their nature has remained relatively unacknowledged and unattended to until modern times.

Have I said yet why, though a man, I decided to complete this chapter after all? No? Well, it was partly because I don't think most women have done so well in writing about the feminine, either. Jung noted this phenomenon half a century ago and attributed it to the fact that neither man nor woman knows much about the soul.[3] Another reason why I am trying to address this topic is because before our eyes, with breathtaking swiftness, a revolution is being accomplished in women's consciousness and in the relationship between

---

[2] Jer. 1:5, RSV.

[3] Jung, "Foreword to Harding: *The Way of All Women,*" *The Symbolic Life,* CW 18, pars. 1795ff.

the sexes. This revolution is having immediate and drastic effects upon us all. The necessary dialogue between women and men on this subject has been lacking for the men have lately been struck dumb. I hope to help repair that imbalance because each sex grieves for the other's suffering, and in humanity's struggle for a new and conscious symbiosis we require the compensatory perspective of the other.

The Special Role of the Feminine in the Coming Age

The Pope in 1950 affirmed what had been the "pious belief of the masses for more than 1000 years,"[4] with his promulgation of the *Assumptio Mariae,* the dogma that the Blessed Virgin Mary has been assumed into heaven body and soul and established as Queen of Heaven and Earth, the equal of God the Father, the Son and the Holy Spirit.[5] Jung says this signifies "the integration of the female principle into the Christian conception of the Godhead . . . certainly the most important religious development for 400 years."[6]

Psychologically the elevation of Mary into heaven, her new status as goddess, means that mankind is preparing to accord highest worth to the feminine principle. In the feminine principle I include the following values which may occur in either women or men, but with which in the past women have been more identified:[7] the heart, the personal, feeling (in particular introverted feeling, as exemplified by Mary of Bethany),[8] the body, life, relatedness, nature, matter, particularity, ordinariness, egohood. It is these principles, with Mary, which are now being borne up to heaven.

Jung writes of Mary:

---

[4] Jung, *Letters,* vol. 2, p. 206.
[5] *Encyclical Ad Caeli Reginam,* Oct. 11, 1954.
[6] *Letters,* vol. 1, p. 567.
[7] See below, chapter 11.
[8] See above, chapter 4, "Mary and Martha."

One could have known for a long time that there was a deep longing in the masses for an intercessor and mediatrix who would at last take her place alongside the Holy Trinity and be received as the "Queen of Heaven and Bride at the Heavenly Court." For more than a thousand years it had been taken for granted that the Mother of God dwelt there, and we know from the Old Testament that Sophia was with God before the creation.[9]

Sophia (Wisdom) is God's feminine counterpart who was forgotten during the Hebrew and Christian dispensations and is now, in the Psychological dispensation, destined to reappear. Jung writes,

> The reappearance of Sophia in the heavenly regions points to a coming act of creation. She is indeed the "master workman"; she realizes God's thoughts by clothing them in material form, which is the prerogative of all feminine beings. Her coexistence with Yahweh signifies the perpetual *hieros gamos* from which worlds are begotten and born. A momentous change is imminent: God desires to regenerate himself in the mystery of the heavenly nuptials—as the chief gods of Egypt had done from time immemorial—and to become man. For this he uses the Egyptian model of the god's incarnation in Pharaoh, which in its turn is but a copy of the eternal *hieros gamos* in the pleroma.[10]

When a major transformation of consciousness is to take place, it takes the form of a conception and a birth. In the Egyptian model it was the Pharaoh, part God, part man, who incarnated God. In the Christian dispensation, God, incarnate in his son, was born of Mary. Now, in the new dispensation, we are all to be incarnators of the divine.

Jung, alone of his generation, understood the psychological significance of the *Assumptio Mariae,* that it was "intended to compensate the truly apocalyptic world situation today,"[11] and that it marked the installation of the feminine principle alongside the masculine as heavenly or guiding principles. By its deification the feminine is now

---

9 "Answer to Job," *Psychology and Religion,* CW 11, par. 748.

10 Ibid., par. 624.

11 Ibid., par. 749.

accorded the esteem it deserves and its equality with the masculine is secured. The *Assumptio,* because it implies the *hieros gamos* (sacred marriage) foretells

> the future birth of the divine child, who, in accordance with the divine trend towards incarnation, will choose as his birthplace the empirical man. [This] metaphysical process is known to the psychology of the unconscious as the individuation process.[12]

Gerhard Adler equates God's calling upon his helpmeet Sophia to his calling on the Eros side of his nature. He writes:

> God's Sophia appears as the principle of the future, as highest authority, that which can revitalize and transcend an obsolescent and rigidifying concept of God. It is no mere chance that "Answer to Job," with its inherent avowal of Sophia, is Jung's most personal and human book.[13]

Adler believes that in Jung's emphasis on the feminine (yin, Eros), and indeed in his operating from it, he "has initiated an historic change of accent, the importance of which we can as yet hardly grasp."[14]

An outstanding characteristic of the coming age of the Psychological dispensation will be the enthronement of the feminine principle and the revaluation of its primary carrier, woman. Then may be fulfilled the words of the prophet Jeremiah, which can be read as predicting a leadership role for women in our era: "The Lord has created a new thing on the earth; a woman protects a man."[15]

It is fitting that the Psychological dispensation should coincide with the accession of woman to her rightful place as co-equal of man. For she has an affinity to the psyche and to experience. She has been forced into an acquaintanceship with subjective experience because in the outer world she has until lately been rendered powerless. She has been associated with "materiality" as the male has with

---

[12] Ibid., par. 755.
[13] "Aspects of Jung's Personality and Work," p. 19.
[14] Ibid., p. 20.
[15] Jer. 31:22, RSV.

spirituality, but the spirituality of the coming age will be one in which material and spiritual, heart and head, body and mind, woman and man, stand in a relationship of complementarity and equality.

It is women, as a rule, who display more vulnerability, who less frequently "stonewall," who accept their neediness and dependence which are common human properties (though in men, usually outside awareness), who continue as beginners, learners, seekers. To be open to a new beginning means to be capable of psychic transformation, because a readiness to begin anew suggests a readiness to let the old attitude die. This is the inner meaning of death and resurrection. We must be ready to let something die for a new potential in us to be born. As the *I Ching* says, "That a new beginning follows after every ending, is the course of heaven."[16]

While trying to define what I mean by the feminine I have wondered if it is perhaps not everything that has been slighted, discounted and devalued under the hegemony of the masculine principle—silence, introverted feeling,[17] receptivity, instinctuality, earthly delights, concrete reality, work with the hands.

Recently, in Yugoslavia, a group of several children (a male among them) had a vision of Mary. One of the children reported that when she asked Mary why they had been chosen Mary replied that it was because they were ordinary. What a compensation for the masculine heroic ideal!

The following dream of a woman physician illustrates the degradation of the feminine principle in our time. The dreamer is summoned to examine a woman who, all her life, has been imprisoned, battered and abused and is reputed to be crazed and dangerous. The dreamer lifts the emaciated patient (who is lying in a fetal position) in her arms to lay her down gently in order to listen to her heart. The dreamer continues:

> I can see the terror in her face and I have the sense that she is like a vicious animal and may attack me at any time. I ask her permission

---

16 Richard Wilhelm, trans., *The I Ching or Book of Changes*, p. 478.

17 Cordelia in *King Lear* is a good example of the introverted feeling type.

to listen to her heart, then gently lift her gown, revealing no more than is necessary to place the stethoscope, so that she will not feel invaded or that I do not respect her privacy. Her face and entire body soften with relief and she allows the examination. I come away with the awareness that she is very ill. . . . Her name is Mary and I realize that she is, in fact, the Blessed Virgin Mary.[18]

While undeniably partaking of the dreamer's personal psychology this dream just as undeniably must have a collective reference.

I don't mean to attribute characteristics, positive or negative, to the feminine. Women are all too familiar with limiting male definitions of them. Although all women (and men) are influenced by the secret workings of the feminine, I am speaking about an archetype not about women in their flesh and blood reality. Women live the masculine and feminine principles in a womanly way. Men live them in a way that befits a man.[19]

Still Another Creation Story

In the beginning all was one, formless and void. Then with the light (Genesis 1:3), or the serpent (Genesis 3), or the word (John 1:1) or consciousness (Jung's interpretation), the world came into being.

The moment the original unconscious wholeness came into the light it was shown to consist of an infinite array of pairs of opposites, most prominently male and female, spirit and matter, good and evil. The males seized upon one side of each polarity and projected with love and hate the contrary upon the other (woman).[20] Now women have returned to us men the half of our nature that we projected—a gift and an affliction. The question for us men is what do we do with it. Women have said "We are not that." The ball is in our court.

---

[18] Reported by Lionel Corbett, "The Archetypal Feminine: A Response to Betty Meador's Paper at Ghost Ranch, June 1988."

[19] I am indebted to Gareth Hill's lecture, "Masculine and Feminine," for elucidating this point.

[20] See below, chapter 11.

It is easier to speak of the decline of the leading idea under which we have been living than to try to formulate the new one which is coming to birth. Science and rationalism ruled the era now in eclipse and conceived all things as accessible to brainpower. The new ruling idea which we are here calling the feminine principle has to do with restoring the mystery of life. One of the hallmarks of Jungian analysis is acceptance of its lack of knowledge. Keenly aware of the limitations of the intellect, it proffers a sense of the illimitable mysteries of everyday life and thereby makes a place for the feminine.

Jung called the religious attitude careful consideration of the numinous. "Numinous" means something which moves by itself and therefore gives the ego the terrifying and awesome experience of the "wholly other."[21] In this context it refers to our recognition that in psychic life there arc forces that have a life of their own. We don't control them; at best we have a more or less conscious relationship to them—relationship, not knowledge in the sense of the ability to control or predict.

Women, in general, have more interest in psychology and a more natural relationship to it. Women's devoted attention to the unfolding of their individuation process often seems purer than that of men, who more frequently, even while in analysis, have their eye out for worldly advancement of one sort or another. Women are more willing to be learners; in the Buddhist phrase they have a "beginner's mind."[22] This is the religious attitude.

Jung says that woman desires to make her life understandable to herself.[23] What finer example of the religious attitude? Erich Neumann said that the fruit of a man's individuation is knowledge, while a woman's is transformation.[24] Or put another way, "Man does, woman is." The affinity between woman and being recalls the

---

[21] See Edward F. Edinger, *Melville's Moby-Dick: A Jungian Commentary,* p. 149. The word numinous was coined by Rudolph Otto in *The Idea of the Holy.*

[22] Suzy J. Spradlin, personal communication.

[23] *Letters,* vol. 1, p. 151.

[24] *The Child,* p. 192.

philosophies of the East and supports the theory that in the Psychological dispensation woman will have achieved her element.

Yeats writes, "The intellect of man is forced to choose/ Perfection of the life or of the work."[25] For millennia women have chosen perfection of the life. But this does not produce a cultural artifact, neither a book nor a statue, nor a religion, nor a road, nor even a poem or a piece of music. For millennia the poetry and the music emanating from the souls of women have been memorialized in the lives of their sons.

Consider the art of dance. While the great majority of its practitioners are women, in the subfield of choreography (which attempts to give permanent form to that ephemeral art) men predominate. So deeply immersed is woman in the living moment, and so tender and attuned is her devotion to the God who is incarnating among us in that moment, that she counts it an injury to that relationship to wrench away her full presence by the mechanical act of recording. More than men she has been aware, in Rilke's words, of "an ancient enmity between our daily life and the great work."[26] Thus it is that she has produced fewer tangible cultural products than men.

With astonishing prescience Rilke wrote the following in 1904:

> [Women] in their new, individual unfolding, will only in passing be imitators of masculine behavior and misbehavior and repeaters of masculine professions. After the uncertainties of such transitions it will become obvious that women were only going through the profusion and the vicissitude of those (often ridiculous) disguises in order to cleanse their own essential nature of the distorting influences of the other sex.
>
> Women, in whom life lingers and dwells more immediately, more fruitfully and more confidently, must surely have become fundamentally riper people, more human people, than lightly-going man, who is not pulled down below the surface of life by the weight of any fruit of his body, and who, presumptuous and hasty, undervalues what he thinks he loves.

---

25 "The Choice," in *Collected Poems of W.B. Yeats.*
26 "Requiem for a Friend," in *The Selected Poetry of Rainer Maria Rilke,* p. 87.

This humanity of woman, borne its full time in suffering and humiliation, will come to light when she will have cast off the conventions of mere femininity in her outward status, and those men who do not yet feel it approaching today will be surprised and struck by it. Someday . . . there will be women whose name will no longer signify merely an opposite of the masculine, but something in itself, something that makes one think, not of any complement and limit, but only of life and reality: the feminine human being.

This advance will (at first much against the will of the outstripped men) change the love-experience, which is now full of error, will alter it from the ground up, reshape it into a relation that is meant to be of one human being to another, no longer of man to woman. And this more human love (that will fulfill itself, infinitely considerate and gentle, and kind and clear in binding and releasing) will resemble that which we are preparing with struggle and toil, the love that consists in this: that two solitudes protect and touch and greet each other.[27]

Erich Neumann, one of the most original of Jung's followers, attempted to characterize the peculiar nature of feminine (matriarchal) consciousness. Unlike masculine consciousness, for which understanding is an act of "swift registration, development and organization" performed by the intellect,[28] for feminine consciousness understanding is like a conception which needs time and shelter to come to term. "Whatever is to be understood," Neumann writes of feminine consciousness, "must first 'enter' matriarchal consciousness in the full, sexual, symbolic meaning of a fructification."[29] Pursuing the metaphor of feminine understanding as conception, pregnancy and birth, Neumann writes as follows:

To "carry" a knowledge and allow it to ripen means, at the same time, to "accept" it; and acceptance, which here includes the idea of "assimilation," is a typically feminine form of activity, not to be confused with passive submission or drifting. The comparative passivity of matriarchal consciousness is not due to any incapacity for

---

[27] *Letters to a Young Poet,* pp. 76-78 (modified).
[28] "On the Moon and Matriarchal Consciousness," in *Five Papers on the Archetypal Background of Family Psychology,* p. 47.
[29] Ibid.

action, but rather to an awareness of subjection to a process in which it can "do" nothing, but can only "let happen." In all decisive life situations, the feminine, to a far greater degree than the nothing-but-masculine, is subjected to the numinous elements in nature or, still better, has these "brought home" to it. Therefore, its relation to nature and to God is more familiar and intimate, and its tie to an anonymous transpersonal allegiance forms earlier and goes deeper than its personal tie to a man.

Although matriarchal consciousness exists in all human beings and plays an important role in men, especially if they are creative, women are still the real representatives of this consciousness, even now when they have a patriarchal consciousness at their disposal too, and the opposition between the two attitudes has become a source of deep conflict. For woman has held the attitude of receptivity and acceptance, which is basic to matriarchal consciousness, since the beginning of time. She takes this attitude for granted. It is not only during the menstrual period that, to live wisely, she must place her harmony with the moon above the desires and plans of the masculine side of her ego-consciousness. Pregnancy and birth bring total psycho-biological changes also, demanding and presupposing adaptations and adjustments lasting for years on end. In regard to the unknown nature of the child, its character, its sex—a matter of decisive importance in many cultures, both matriarchal and patriarchal—its health, its fate, in all these things, woman is delivered over to the mercy and power of God, and condemned, as an ego, to helpless non-activity and non-intervention.[30]

It is the feminine principle then, and all it symbolizes, that appears to be destined to mediate the new consciousness that desires to be born in our time.

The Feminine Realizes and Embodies the Spirit

Jung said it is the function of the feminine to clothe spirit in material form. In the first, the Hebrew, dispensation, Eve received God in the Garden of Eden in the form of the serpent. The divinely stamped portion of mankind began with Adam and Eve. Jung says that the

---

[30] Ibid., p. 52

Israelites are like a bride to God who jealously watched over their faithfulness.[31]

In the second, the Christian dispensation, Mary received the Holy Spirit. Eve's acceptance of the serpent and Mary's obedience to God at the Annunciation are two aspects of the same event which may be "perceived as opposites because they occur at different stages of ego development."[32]

In the third, the Psychological dispensation, each of us, through our feminine side, will receive the Holy Spirit and God will be conceived in us.

In each case it is the feminine which conceives the new ruling principle and in each case what she does is at first a shock to the masculine (Adam, Joseph and in our day men in general).

The encounter with a snake, as in the Garden of Eden myth, symbolizes the call to individuation.[33] The snake is fearful and uncanny—it enters one's life without warning and is capable of transforming it decisively. Its bite, understood as a sort of conception, is in accord with its phallic significance.

A mythologem related to that of the call to individuation (or initiation) is that of being offered something to eat. Edinger says the general rule is, if in a dream you are offered something to eat, then eat.[34] According to this idea, then, our ancestress Eve was wise to accept the fruit offered her by the serpent.

In the more ancient Biblical version of the creation, man is created first and woman is created from his rib.[35] Why the rib? Perhaps because of the male's sense of woman as being connected to him via his feelings (the rib comes from the heart region). Men's unconsciousness of their feminine side is highlighted by the fact that God

---

[31] "Answer to Job," *Psychology and Religion,* CW 11, par. 616.

[32] Edward F. Edinger, *The Christian Archetype: A Jungian Commentary on the Life of Christ,* p. 26.

[33] Ibid., p. 26.

[34] *Anatomy of the Psyche: Alchemical Symbolism in Psychotherapy,* p. 111.

[35] Gen. 2: 21-22.

put Adam to sleep during this operation. This story also hints at men's and women's essential androgyny.[36]

In another creation story Adam and his first wife, Lilith, were created together and according to one version they were Siamese twins, joined back to back. Lilith refused to accept Adam's authority and hence she was driven from Paradise, becoming the bride of the Devil and the mother of demons. Edinger says this legend personifies the idea, so prevalent in our day, of the offended feminine principle.[37]

We seem to be returning now to the myth of the androgyne (witness the increasing boyishness of girls and feminization of boys). Progressing with great swiftness this collective movement of the spirit seems to have as its goal a new kind of human consciousness—one that is adequate to the perils and problems of contemporary life. This new consciousness will relinquish the old image of conflict-resolution by means of "settling the other's hash." On this small planet, in this one world, that outmoded model of conflict resolution through the exercise of power, a characteristic of patriarchy, no longer serves. Indeed, among thoughtful young people the use of power to achieve ego purposes grows increasingly abhorrent.

That the depiction of violence is so prevalent in the media is not so much a measure of its elemental attractiveness as an indication that our relationship to violence is beginning to emerge into consciousness. The first and most important step in that process is ruling it out as an option in real life, thus relegating it to the psychological realm where it is accessible to an inner transformative process. What is substituted for physical violence and other applications of power is Eros, understanding, communication—the psychological mode. As Jung says, "Where love reigns, there is no will to power; and where the will to power is paramount, love is lacking."[38]

---

[36] Edward F. Edinger, *The Bible and the Psyche: Individuation Symbolism in the Old Testament,* p. 20.

[37] "Yahweh and Individuation," public program, C.G. Jung Institute, San Francisco, 1980.

[38] *Two Essays on Analytical Psychology,* CW 7, par. 78.

In contrast to the lowly station accorded woman in the outer world she seems to have a readier access to the psyche. More than men, she seems disposed to realize and embody ideals and concepts. For the famed mythologist Joseph Campbell, who taught for years at Sarah Lawrence, it came as a revelation that his students (all women) should insist on knowing what these myths had to say for their everyday lives. Their desire, to relate the transcendent or mythic dimension to immediate life experience, was identical with that of Meister Eckhart who spoke these words at his Christmas sermon:

> Here in time we make holiday because the eternal birth which God the Father bore and bears unceasingly in eternity is now borne in time, in human nature. St. Augustine says this birth is always happening. But if it happen not in me, what does it profit me? What matters is that it shall happen in me. We intend therefore to speak of this birth as happening in us, as being consummated in the virtuous soul; for it is in the perfect soul that God speaks his Word . . . There is a saying of the wise man: "When all things were in the midst of silence, then leapt there down into me from on high, from the royal throne, a secret Word."[39]

In other words an idea may be of little consequence unless it is realized in experience.

A Clinical Example: Elise's Dream

The following is the dream of a highly intelligent, extraverted young woman who was in the throes of a marriage problem:

> It was night-time and I was lying on my bed but it was raised so that I could look out the window. I watched as a light in the sky began to move and swiftly approached me. I did not know whether to be frightened but my dog barked happily at it which reassured me. The light seemed to enter into me, settling in my heart region. Now it was like a small candle flame. I knew it would always be with me and I could turn to it for warmth whenever I needed it.

---

[39] Quoted by Jung in *Mysterium Coniunctionis,* par. 444n.

I told her that with such a dream she need never be overly anxious about the vicissitudes of her outer life.

To the light that descended, taking up residence in her heart, she had two associations, the moon and a dove. The moon is symbolic of the feminine principle and the dove is the bird of Aphrodite, the goddess of love, as well as a symbol of reconciliation and of the Holy Spirit. I told her how the Holy Spirit, in contrast to what is often taught, had feminine connotations.

In this connection Edinger has cited Yeats' "Mother of God" poem, which refers to a shooting star that, as in my patient's dream, takes root in the flesh. "What is this flesh I purchased with my pains/ This fallen star my milk sustains?"[40] Elsewhere Edinger comments,

> According to ancient thinking the moon, as the "planet" closest to earth, was the gateway between the celestial and the earthly realms. All spiritual entities on the way to embodiment were funnelled through the moon where they were materialized.[41]

At first the dream impressed me more than it did the dreamer. She worked in a results-oriented profession. What the dream was offering her, she felt, was a mere semblance that suffered by comparison with "real" achievement. She felt dreams to be as deficient in value as they were in substance. What the dream was offering her she termed "second-best."

In fact, the dream presented to this woman the possibility of finding a connection to an emotional, though invisible, truth which could grant her much of what she most deeply yearned for. The dove had come to her as a symbol of reconciliation (that is why it has come to symbolize peace). But she understood what she was being offered as a poor substitute for the real thing. Highly extraverted, she had fallen prey to the cultural disparagement of the invisible world. But through its effect on her analyst she was enabled, in some degree, to take seriously the dream symbols which in turn allowed the dream to have a

---

[40] "The Christian Archetype," public program, C.G. Jung Institute, San Francisco, 1980.
[41] *Anatomy of the Psyche,* p. 96.

healing effect. The dream can be understood as a fulfillment of Jesus' assurance:

> The Advocate, the Holy Spirit whom the Father will send in my name will teach you everything and remind you of all I have said to you. Peace I bequeath to you, my own peace I give you, a peace the world cannot give, this is my gift to you. Do not let your hearts be troubled or afraid.[42]

Despite this woman's initial skepticism, as the years passed she was granted in some measure the peace she had intuited in the dream.

---

[42] John 14:26-27, JB.

11
Women and Men in the
Psychological Dispensation

No one has yet gone out into the streets to celebrate [the death of
the patriarchy] perhaps because people were afraid that if they
made too much noise they would bring the dead back to life; perhaps too because man's disarray touches women to the heart.
—Elizabeth Badinter, *The Unopposite Sex.*

The Projection Upon Women

We are entering an age in which Jung's myth of the "ongoing
incarnation of God for the purpose of divine transformation" is
beginning to take hold in the lives of individuals. In no aspect of our
experience is the impact of this new consciousness more apparent
than in the relationship between the sexes.

In order to realize their own essential nature uncontaminated by
the prejudices of society, women more and more desire men to withdraw their projections. (Women are not always wholehearted or consistent in this desire and sometimes collude with men in a system of
mutual projections, but this chapter confines itself to the case of
men's projections upon women.) Men cannot at once cease their
projections upon women, because whatever is unconscious is projected and woman literally personifies (in dreams and fantasies) the
unconscious of man.

What men *can* do is examine their projections. I try to do that in
this final chapter while, for purposes of discussion, continuing to attribute characteristics to the feminine and to women. Alongside those
attributions I place a mental question mark.

In any event all this talk about masculine and feminine may be
away from the real point, which is that when a psychic content (in

149

this case the Self) newly surfaces into consciousness, it divides into pairs of opposites because our ego cannot apprehend at once all sides of an emerging wholeness. The aspect of our nature which remains unconscious is projected upon the opposite sex.

One distinctive half of this array of pairs of opposites has been projected upon the feminine and (for the most part) disparaged. Now we are experiencing the return of those values repressed and devalued by men and our patriarchal society. Most of the words that supposedly characterize the feminine suggest inferiority—sometimes subtly. So the masculine and men have become equated with superiority. We men must reclaim as our own what we have projected upon women, and by consciously attending to those values burn away the inferiority which has clung to them.

Let us examine, for example, the polarity independence/dependence. Undeniably, "independence" has a better ring to it. Men have been insufficiently aware of their dependence, including their dependence upon women, and have compounded that error by characterizing women as dependent. Unclear about their own dependence they are hindered in coming to terms with it. Rilke says that men "undervalue what they think they love."[1] They are also unconscious of it.

For men, women carry traits such as dependence, which is part of human nature and necessary for life. This enables men to benefit (through contact with women) from the life-sustaining energies of nature, while simultaneously disparaging those values (for example, dependence) in comparison with the goal-oriented activities to which they devote their conscious attention, gathering treasures on earth for themselves and those "they think they love." Men's achievements thereby support their illusion of independence.

It is becoming clear that we men have been projecting upon women valuable and rejected parts of our own nature. The time has come to begin consciously retrieving these parts of ourselves for three reasons: 1) to relieve women of the burden of carrying alone characteristics that belong to both sexes, thus freeing them to carry

---

[1] *Letters to a Young Poet,* p. 77.

forward the work of the God which is incarnating in them; 2) to reclaim lost portions of our own souls which, in the past, we have experienced mainly through women; and 3) in order to preserve the world in this way: through beginning to discern in ourselves that sensitivity, softness, innocence, earthiness, charm, love of life, grace, receptivity and attunement with nature, which may result in our treating the earth and each other with more consideration.

Discovering within ourselves a whole world which we had projected outside—a world of care and sensitivity—we will, perhaps, be convinced of the reality and the unconditional right to exist of all things that grow (including feelings that grow within us) and thus we may be moved to conserve and protect them. These newly discovered feelings will perhaps serve as a counterbalance to men's traditional competitiveness, warlikeness and exploitiveness—traits men have generally carried for women.

The slate must be wiped clean—no attributions to the other sex. Certainly projections will continue to fly. These must be examined. This is the agenda for couples in the new age, for the Psychological dispensation demands that men and women become conscious of both their masculine and feminine components.

In the work of undoing projections women are ahead of their male counterparts for a number of reasons:

1) They are generally more psychological.

2) Because of the alleged superiority of the masculine they have been more accepting of the contrasexual side of their nature than men (thus, as often happens, an inferiority in the outer world is converted into a blessing in the inner).

3) Women fear being turned into men less than men fear the ancient bugaboo.

4) Living in a patriarchal society for millennia has offered women opportunities aplenty to acquaint themselves with the workings of the masculine principle which is, for instance, the main preoccupation of all schooling.

5) Whatever the feminine may be, it is harder to grasp in the masculine ways we are all so well acquainted with, mainly words, logic, concepts, analysis.

Receptivity

> You loved me before the foundation of the world.[2]

Another trait which has been carried extensively by women is that of receptivity, which does not sound quite so estimable as its opposite—activity—frequently attributed to men.

In a letter to Aniela Jaffé, Jung describes in these moving words his experience of a paper of his being "received":

> I thank you with all my heart for your response. . . . I could not imagine a more beautiful one. It is a "total" reaction, and it had a "total" effect on me too. You have perfectly imaged what I imagined into my work. It again became clear to me . . . how much one misses when one receives no response or a mere fragment, and what a joy it is to experience the opposite—a creative resonance which is at the same time a revelation of the feminine being. It is as though a wine, which by dint of toil and sweat, worry and care, has finally become mature and good, were poured into a precious beaker. Without this receptacle and acceptance a man's work remains a delicate child, followed with doubting eyes and released into the world with inner anxiety. But when a soul opens to the work, it as though a seed were lodged in good earth, or the gates of a city were closed in the evening, so that it can enjoy surer repose. I thank you.[3]

In order to relieve women of the inferiority which, as our patriarchal inheritance, still adheres to the term "receptacle," no alternative is left but for us men to claim it as our own, because it certainly also belongs to our own nature.

Being a receptacle or receiving another is equivalent to what psychotherapists call mirroring, that is, reflecting back to another the

---

[2] John 17:24, JB.
[3] *Letters,* vol. 1, p. 474.

other's conscious experience. On a deeper level mirroring means receiving, registering and reflecting back to the other their hidden essence or potential of which they were only dimly aware and which can make its appearance in the world only as the result of someone's having glimpsed it.

Nothing is so precious or sought after as being mirrored, received by another human being. Sometimes inexperienced psychotherapists tell me they feel at a loss when their patients devalue their profession—for therapists offer themselves as mirrors, as receptacles. Perhaps the patients question how so precious a commodity (akin to love) could be for sale, so to speak. The fact is that you can't quite buy it—what you can purchase is the opportunity for this receiving to take place. If it happens at all it is a mutual thing, occurring as a function of the relationship between patient and therapist and in no way the product of anyone's will.

I once had a patient who, far from receiving me, habitually misrepresented and discredited me. I found (to my surprise and frustration) that I in my turn could not receive her, though I knew she needed it badly. And so I discovered that my functioning as a receptacle was not something I could bestow upon anyone. Rather it was something that was evoked in the meeting of two consciousnesses, or not.

Women's Relationship to the Masculine

Today we are witnessing a revolution of world-shaking proportions—the revolution in women's consciousness. Women are seeing the world with their own eyes, neither seeking harmony with men's world view nor reacting as much in anger to it.

Woman has been angry because much in her essential nature has been held in low esteem. What is worse, she herself seems at times to have been won over to the pernicious ethos of our time—the overvaluing of worldly power and the undervaluing of its compensation, the kingdom which is "not of this world," the inner world. Thus woman has been set at war with her own nature. Like her brother she has come to overvalue thinking (Logos) and undervalue feeling (Eros).

The "inferiority" of the feminine is largely based on its being equated with the feeling function which, in its introverted guise at least, is universally considered secondary to thinking. Future generations will look back at our era and see that in our emphasis on the intellect since the French Enlightenment we were off the mark. What we were aiming at was really the wisdom which apprehends the whole, combining masculine and feminine, thinking and feeling. We have suffered through two centuries of a massive devaluation of the inner world, which corresponds in part with the feminine principle. As Marie-Louise von Franz says, "In our modern world, women have achieved their sexual freedom. . . . Now comes the much bigger problem: the liberation of the heart. That is the program of the next fifty years."[4]

Men have failed in their immemorial task of upholding the spiritual point of view, hence the torch of the spirit has passed to women.

In the past woman has mainly sought fulfillment through relationship: husband, children, family. For bad and good reasons she has sought, especially in the last generation, to withdraw some of her energies from these pursuits. Bad reasons have to do with her acceptance of destructive (when misplaced) masculine values such as the "bottom line" mentality. Positive reasons have to do with her rejection of the conventional expectation of wife-and-mother as the one and only role for woman.

Women have in fact had to adopt Logos values to function at all in most work places. Participation in activities of an impersonal nature is just as important as personal relationship for a woman's development.[5] This is why (other than for obvious economic reasons) many women seek work outside the home. Paradoxically, impersonal work often nourishes her femininity, for her feminine nature comes into flower too as she makes use of all sides of herself. Genuine

---

4 *The Way of the Dream,* p. 299.
5 Jane Wheelwright, *Feminine Spirit,* unpublished manuscript.

femininity seems to be linked to a woman's development of her potential. What a contrast with Susan Brownmiller's definition of femininity: "The feminine principle is composed of vulnerability, the need for protection, the formalities of compliance and the avoidance of conflict."[6]

I knew a woman who in her seventies blossomed in every way. She found her "voice" and her self-confidence, and stepping forth into the world for the first time as herself, she released a fragrant and alluring feminine loveliness. I realized clearly, then, that feminine beauty and charm were as much psychic as physical.

I have asked myself, "Why the extraordinary responsiveness of women to male expectations?" Are women, more than men, social creatures and thus more influenced by social expectations? Though women may not like my saying so, I believe that there is a constitutional factor which disposes them to accept the projections of another person.[7] Perhaps it is greater relatedness based on the primordial necessity of relating to children. Perhaps it is the knowledge in her flesh of the essential oneness of things.

The Relationship Between the Sexes in the Psychological Dispensation

What will happen when men and women cease projecting upon each other so much? Or rather what will become of us when we begin seeing in ourselves characteristics previously relegated to the other sex? How the ground will move beneath our feet—or do I already feel the shaking?

How will things look when men begin to notice written upon their own souls what they had formerly projected upon women? After the terror and the turmoil of this disillusionment will likely arise a recognition of the sanctity of the individuation process as it reveals itself in

---

[6] *On Femininity,* p. 16.

[7] Some research on gender differences in infants supports this view. See, for example, Doris K. Silverman, "What Are Little Girls Made Of?"

the other: admiration and respect for God's work unfolding in one you love. And men may realize that their conscious and unconscious devaluation of women corresponds point-by-point to the devaluation of their own souls.

Why do I claim that spiritual leadership has now passed to woman? Because courageously she is forcing men to drop their projections upon her. Willingly she begins to sacrifice the power she once wielded by virtue of those same projections. Much power accrued to women, for example, through men's erotic desire for them. Many modern women now prefer to put their energies elsewhere than cultivating and exploiting those "feminine" allurements.

Some men will feel disappointed and deprived by the growing independence and autonomy of women, their withdrawal of the maternal virtues of self-sacrifice, protectiveness and submission. But missed most of all, perhaps, will be women's admiration, recognition and respect.

Woman will no longer be expected to subordinate herself to man. She will no longer be expected to put a man and his needs before her own, or align herself with his purposes, applaud his successes and grieve for his failures, while neglecting her own.

In the days when women cared more for men it was not (though it seemed to be) for the man himself she cared, but for the principles men had brought forth and stood for and served day and night. It was not for her husband, but for God, that a woman subordinated herself. She subordinated herself for the sake of the family and community which nourished her and which was of the highest value, more important than her husband's personality or her own. We must all have something greater than ourselves to live for.

In return for this loss of support, men will be privileged to witness the green shoots of the Holy Spirit pushing upward in the soil of women's consciousness. And this will be in keeping with the immemorial calling of men to serve the spirit in whatever guise (however inconvenient or even terrifying) it manifests itself. To subordinate himself to the spirit as it takes form in the souls and hearts and minds of women would be once more to enter into battle. This seems an heroic task—worthy of a man. Let us remember how Heracles for three years served Queen Omphale who adorned him in petticoats and set him spinning and sewing while she, dressed in his lion skins, wielded his truncheon. For a man to accept his feminine nature cannot help but threaten his identity as a man. Yet that is precisely the heroic task that faces us men. We are Sophia, Mary, Lilith, Kali, Kundry.

In former times women often placed the lives of others before their own. Now it may be our turn, as men, to honor (with the sacrifice of our energies—our lives, if necessary) those upon whom the burden of carrying the spirit has fallen. To do so is to join women in their love and obeisance to God. In the words of Mary, "Let what you have said be done to me."[8]

Do you know the story of the young king Admetus who, summoned by Death, first tried to bargain, then screamed out as his mother once did in childbirth?

Alarmed, his aged parents appeared at his side. He asked that they substitute for him, then beseeched his best friend, for it had been ordained that if he found a substitute, Death would pass him by. All, however, preferred to cling to whatever shred of life was left them except his wife, Alcestis, who stepped forward unasked. She, his friend and helpmeet, claimed the right to stand hostage for him. And so Death took her.

We men, if necessary, must do as Alcestis did—stand ransom for our beloved—subordinate ourselves to her, for we and our sister are one and suffer as one. Our souls, our hearts, cry out in unison. At this moment in history our sister is, in some respects, clearer and more urgent about the problem. She is in the front line, in the trenches. (I am deliberately using images that speak to men, attempting to give us something worth fighting for.)

We must support woman's struggle because it is ours as well— and because our hearts swell in admiration for her heroism and remember her sacrifices, forgiving her those occasions when, battling

---

[8] Luke 1:38, JB.

so valiantly and (she thinks) alone, for a small moment she mistakes us for the enemy.

Being a Man in the New Dispensation

How have we gotten into this? We men, guardians of the spirit (in the patriarchal tradition) have failed in our sacred duty. Where, except in women, can we see the spirit at work in our time?

What do I mean by spirit, you ask? The spirit is what makes life meaningful. If it is accepted that man lives not by bread alone, by what *does* man live? And what in the way of meaning do men have to offer those who cannot live by making a bundle alone. It is impossible, any more, to be poor with dignity. Nothing is left worth fighting or dying for. We are spiritually bankrupt. (Isn't this obvious yet?) Even patriotism, that last refuge of scoundrels, no longer suffices, even for scoundrels. So what have we? Science?—too narrow. Liberalism, so called humanitarianism?—full of unconscious righteousness and self-delusion (including projections of our dark and needy soul upon other peoples). Religions (like liberalism), which don't know they're religions, in the long run turn destructive to mankind (as Communism has.)

We men do not know any more what it is to be a man. In that respect my father failed me and I have failed my sons. As a teenager my oldest son liked to think that men were better drivers than women. Quoting contradictory statistics muzzled him but I don't think he gave up the notion. I understood his opinion to be a desperate attempt to gain some identity as a male by distinguishing himself from women (especially his sister).

Men would fall all over themselves in their haste to learn from a man who knew how to be a man in our day. Instead young men shrink from our spiritually bankrupt school system which at best assists them in finding their niche in a spiritually bankrupt society.

Another of my sons, as a graduating high school senior, chose as the epigram to accompany his photo in the yearbook, Mark Twain's maxim, "I've never let my schooling interfere with my education."

You can't keep young people from learning, but nobody any more seems able to think of a curriculum that offers what they thirst for.

I don't know what that curriculum would be either, but it would surely offer young men and women meaning in life, and it would help them understand how men and women are different—and the ways in which they are similar.

I once asked three acquaintances, two women and a man, if there was any difference between men and women, other than physical. There was a long silence while we all thought about it. Finally one woman came up with, "Men still have more earning power." A man cannot build his identity upon the fact that he has more earning power, especially since his higher earning power is probably not based upon higher productivity but is rather a symptom of our still patriarchal society.

Some say no difference exists any more between men and women except that only women can bear children.[9] With sperm banks, *in vitro* fertilization and other techniques, a male partner is no longer indispensable for procreation. Some call men redundant.

What then can the old men of the tribe offer the young men who need to define themselves? The ceremony that once accomplished this is called initiation, a ritual marking the transition from boyhood to manhood. In Christianity it was confirmation, in Judaism bar mitzvah. But these rites no longer have any effect. The power they once wielded must have been enormous, an unforgettable event in which the initiate's whole life attitude was turned upside down—in other words, he was reborn.

What is left? Mostly pale imitations—driving a car, finishing school, entering the armed services. Combat can still be an important initiation experience—but it is fortunately something which cannot be planned. Who would want their offspring to experience the mortal perils of the battlefield, no matter what transformative experiences they might have there?

---

[9] Elizabeth Badinter, *The Unopposite Sex: The End of the Gender Battle*, p. xiii.

Men primordially have been hunters, warriors, builders of institutions and creators of religions and other spiritual disciplines. But there is little hunting or fighting to be done these days (in fact large segments of our society frown on these activities), and our institutions are mostly morally destitute.

But there is is another primordial function of men. They have traditionally been the purveyors of meaning. Churches once had a function in decanting the Holy Spirit into the cups of thirsting humanity; now they prove their spiritual poverty by their emphasis on socializing and worldly business such as social action (however worthy these causes may be).

Men and women thirst for meaning in their lives as they hunger for food—without both, they die. We are at a period in history when we are deprived of meaning. We suffer and we don't know why, thus we have less strength to endure our suffering. When, lacking meaning, we shrink from the psychic pain, the guilt, the shame and fear, the terror and the loneliness which are all a part of conscious life, we may turn to alcohol or drugs or crime or sex, even to war— anything to give us the feeling that there is something more important in life than our own egos.

So what can fathers do for their children? The rebellion of women against the patriarchy is in part a reaction to the abdication by men of their immemorial task, to devote themselves to the spirit, thereby discovering for humanity principles to live by. We fathers must seek meaning. If we find it for ourselves we may be able to help our children find their path.

A contemporary philosopher recounts that as a young man he yearned for the answer to such questions as, "What is the meaning of life?" and "Is there a God?" These questions were once the acknowledged bedrock of philosophical concerns. He almost changed his mind about his chosen major when, in his introductory philosophy course, he was publicly mocked by the professor for expecting philosophy to answer such questions.

Our schools will not suffice. Nor can we expect our churches to offer up meaning for ourselves or our children. Just as our academic institutions have become hidebound in a narrow conception of science and specialized disciplines, so have our religious institutions become petrified in a nonevolving conception of God. Having lost touch with the Holy Spirit, organized religion, too, has no revelation that speaks to the soul.

The Psychological Dispensation

The kingdom of God is within you.[10]

If we look within we will discover a whole world. If we enter into dialogue with this subjective world we will find guidance as well as a measure of fear and conflict that should not be underestimated.

In other words, in exploring our own nature we will come upon the figures of God and the Devil. We will rediscover Moses' tablets of the law and Jesus' relation to his Father and more—all the terror and turmoil and glory of the Old and New Testament—written upon our hearts.

In this search for the the highest value within us we will need the aid of what the alchemists called their *soror mystica,* their mystical sister who labored beside them over the furnaces. Today, woman, our sister and bride, has claimed her full equality and taken her place at our side. This gives us an opportunity unexampled in history to explore the souls of men and women, for only in the tension of a dialogue of equals can the energy be generated which will transform both.

A man must enter into dialogue with the woman in his life, both in her outer guise as flesh and blood human being and in her inner guise as soul image. In order to be her equal in this work of individuation we men must devote ourselves to an exploration of our inner landscape, as for so many centuries we have explored and analyzed the physical world. For this inner work a different sort of science is required. For a start, we can look for guidance to the new science of

---

[10] Luke 17:21.

depth psychology, which dedicates itself to an exploration of the soul and has the capacity to generate meaning through bridging the gulf between faith and science.

I have a vision of man and woman standing together as equals, joined in their devotion to the God emerging in both. In the past marriage was mainly a social and economic institution. Later it became also an object of romantic projections which, of course, it remains. Because it has become such a troubled institution we begin to understand marriage psychologically, as an image of the union of opposites which are drawn together in love and enmity.[11]

The opposites attract because we unconsciously seek out what we lack. Hence sexuality can be understood as the desire to complete ourselves psychologically as well as physically. According to the Talmud there is rejoicing in heaven at each marital embrace on earth. This can be understood as a restatement of the thesis of this book, that something in the psychic background (we can call it the Self or God) offers us its blessing when we draw closer to that which has remained unconscious to us, that is, when we become more conscious.

Marriage may have no more essential purpose today than the generation of a new consciousness.

---

[11] See Jung, *Mysterium Coniunctionis*, CW 14, par. 1.

Summary

The world is not supposed to work. All it does
effectively is produce consciousness.
    —Robert Johnson, "The Double Animus."

The decisive question for man is: Is he related to something
infinite or not. That is the telling question of his life.
    —C.G.Jung, *Memories, Dreams, Reflections.*

The work of sight is done. Do heart work now.
    —Rainer Maria Rilke, "Turning."

It is the thesis of this book that C.G. Jung will be remembered by
future generations not primarily as the founder of a school of psychotherapy but as one who brought to suffering humanity a new, redemptive understanding which restores meaning to our lives.

What is valuable in Jung's psychology will relatively soon, I
think, be assimilated into the mainstream of depth psychology and
psychotherapy. I refer to such contributions as the treatment of the
patient as an equal, the reverent approach to the psyche, an unequal-
led depth of understanding of dreams, complexes and other unconscious material, and a knowledge of psychological typology.[1] This
will leave still untapped Jung's religious message or metapsycholo-
gy, which the distinguished Jungian analyst Gerhard Adler considered his most important contribution.[2]

Jung's religious (in its widest sense) message, the essence of his
psychology, continues to be overlooked (or misunderstood) even by
some Jungians. Edward Edinger condensed Jung's message into a
single sentence: "Individuation is the ongoing incarnation of God for

---

[1] See *Psychological Types,* CW 6, and Daryl Sharp, *Personality Types:
Jung's Model of Typology.*
[2] "Aspects of Jung's Personality and Work," p. 17.

the purpose of divine transformation."[3] In other words, our human attempt to be as conscious as possible has effects upon the unconscious background of the cosmos. This myth, which was Jung's personal myth, grants unprecedented importance (and therefore meaning) to our actions. This, in a time when the solitary human being (when not acting in concert with a group) is judged of small account.

Why has Jung's message been overlooked? In part because it sounds too much like traditional religion. To the devout it sounds like psychologizing. To those *not* contained in traditional religion, it sounds like regression to a childhood way of looking at things which, with distress and relief, they renounced long ago.

Words like "God" or "Christ" have deep positive or (often in our day) negative childhood associations. These may hamper us from understanding religious images in a more illuminating way, that is, psychologically. Psychological understanding provides the bridge between religion and science. Thus ironically both the religious and the nonreligious, theology and science, have neglected Jung whereas his intention was to create a bridge between them.

If, informed by depth psychology, we reread the scriptures, we discover that they are filled with images and stories still alive in our psyches today. In other words, the Bible is a treasure house of symbolic, not literal, truths. (As the philosopher Owen Barfield pointed out, literalness is idolatry.)[4] These symbolic (read psychic) truths are nonetheless fully real—in fact these truths are the only ones we can know for certain, since modern physics has discovered that matter, whose reality we took for granted, proves ever more insubstantial.

If we accept Jung's and Edinger's translations of Biblical material (with which all Westerners, like it or not, have a conscious or unconscious affinity) into psychological or experiential language, we re-

---

[3] "The Christian Archetype," public program, C.G. Jung Institute, San Francisco, 1980; see also Edinger, *The Bible and the Psyche: Individuation Symbolism in the Old Testament,* p. 11.

[4] *Saving the Appearance: A Study in Idolatry,* pp. 73ff.

ceive a double boon. We are able to understand Jung in a deeper, more feeling way while at the same time the Biblical images, which for many had seemed irrelevant, become imbued with meaning.This psychological language also puts us in touch with the roots of the Western psyche—the collective unconscious.

As we approach the Aquarian age we move under the influence of a new myth, which we here have called the Psychological dispensation.[5] This ruling principle supersedes the Jewish and Christian dispensations, and requires us to forge an individual conscious connection with unconscious contents which in the past were projected in religious images.

In the Jewish dispensation a group, the Israelites, were bound to God in a covenant. In the Christian dispensation a single figure, the God-man Christ, was bound to God as His child. Now, in the Psychological dispensation, we are each bound to God who is incarnating in us. This process is called individuation, the central theme of this book.

My hope, in writing a book as personal as this, was to convey to the reader that the ideas summarized above are not to be taken intellectually only, that Jung's ideas refer to psychic facts which it was his life's work to identify, and that his ideas grant dignity and meaning to the individual only insofar as they are lived or experienced.

---

[5] See above, p. 20.

Bibliography

Adler, Gerhard. "Aspects of Jung's Personality and Work." *Psychological Perspectives,* vol. 6, no. 1 (Spring 1975).

Anderson, Sherwood. *Winesburg, Ohio.* New York: Penguin, 1960.

Badinter, Elizabeth. *The Unopposite Sex: The End of the Gender Battle.* Trans. Barbara Wright. New York: Harper and Row, 1989.

Barfield, Owen. *Saving the Appearance: A Study in Idolatry.* New York: Harcourt, Brace and World, n.d.

Bauer, Jan. *Alcoholism and Women: The Background and the Psychology.* Toronto: Inner City Books, 1982.

Berger, B. "Blind Alley or Road to the Truth?" *New York Times Book Review,* March 31, 1985.

Blake, William. *The Portable Blake.* New York: The Viking Press, 1968.

Brownmiller, Susan. *On Femininity.* New York: Linden Press/Simon and Schuster, 1984.

Carotenuto, Aldo. *The Vertical Labyrinth: Individuation in Jungian Psychology.* Toronto: Inner City Books, 1985.

Corbett, Lionel. "The Archetypal Feminine: A Response to Betty Meador's Paper." Ghost Ranch Conference, June 1988.

Edinger, Edward F. *Anatomy of the Psyche: Alchemical Symbolism in Psychotherapy.* La Salle, IL: Open Court, 1985.

_____. *The Bible and the Psyche: Individuation Symbolism in the Old Testament.* Toronto: Inner City Books, 1986.

_____. "The Christian Archetype." Public Program. C.G. Jung Institute, San Francisco, 1980.

_____. *The Christian Archetype: A Jungian Commentary on the Life of Christ.* Toronto: Inner City Books, 1987.

_____. *The Creation of Consciousness: Jung's Myth for Modern Man.* Toronto: Inner City Books, 1984.

_____. *Ego and Archetype: Individuation and the Religious Function of the Psyche.* New York: Putnam's. 1972.

_____. *Encounter with the Self: A Jungian Commentary on William Blake's Illustrations of the Book of Job.* Toronto: Inner City Books, 1986.

_____. *Melville's Moby-Dick: A Jungian Commentary.* New York: New Directions, 1978.

_____. "Yahweh and Individuation." Public Program. C.G. Jung Institute, San Francisco, 1979.

Eliot, T.S. *The Complete Poems and Plays.* New York: Harcourt Brace, 1952.

Emerson, Ralph Waldo. *Basic Selections from Emerson.* Ed. Eduard Lindeman. New York: New American Library, 1954.

_____. *Essays.* New York: Houghton Mifflin Company, 1883.

Evans, Richard I. *Jung on Elementary Psychology: A Discussion.* New York, E.P. Dutton, 1976.

Freud, Sigmund. *Standard Edition of the Complete Psychological Works,* vol. 16. London: Hogarth Press, 1955.

Gide, André. *The Journals of André Gide.* 3 vols. Trans. Justin O'Brien. London: Secker and Warburg, 1949.

Ginzberg, Louis. *Legends of the Jews.* 7 vols. Philadelphia: Jewish Publication Society, 1909-1938.

Gubitz, Myron B. "Amelek: The Eternal Adversary." In *Psychological Perspectives,* vol. 8, no. 1 (Spring 1977).

Hannah, Barbara. *Jung: His Life and Work.* New York: G.P. Putnam's Sons, 1976.

Hayes, Natalie S. "Matter of Heart." In *Psychological Perspectives,* vol. 14, no. 2 (Fall 1983).

Heschel, Abraham Joshua. *The Sabbath: Its Meaning for Modern Man.* New York: The Noonday Press, 1951.

Hill, Gareth. "Masculine and Feminine." Public Lecture. C. G. Jung Institute of San Francisco, March 28, 1987.

Hitler, Adolf. *Mein Kampf.* Boston: Houghton Mifflin Company, 1973.

Jacoby, Mario. *The Analytic Encounter: Transference and Human Relationship.* Toronto: Inner City Books, 1984.

Jaffé, Aniela. *From the Life and Work of C.G. Jung.* Trans. R.F.C. Hull. New York: Harper and Row, 1968.

_____. *The Myth of Meaning.* Zurich: Daimon Verlag, 1984.

Jensen, Ferne, ed. *C.G. Jung, Emma Jung and Toni Wolff.* San Francisco: Analytical Psychology Club of San Francisco, 1982.

Johnson, Robert. "The Double Animus." Lecture. Friends of Jung, San Diego, CA, October 18, 1978.

Jung, C.G. *The Collected Works* (Bollingen Series XX). 20 vols. Trans. R.F.C. Hull. Ed. H. Read, M. Fordham, G. Adler, Wm. McGuire. Princeton: Princeton University Press, 1953-1979.

_____. *Dream Analysis: Notes of the Seminar Given in 1928-1930* (Bollingen Series XCIX). Ed. Wm. McGuire. Princeton: Princeton University Press, 1984.

_____. "Face to Face: The BBC Interviews." In *Psychological Perspectives,* vol. 7, no. 2 (Fall 1976).

_____. *Letters* (Bollingen Series XCV). 2 vols. Princeton: Princeton University Press, 1973.

_____. *Man and His Symbols.* New York: Doubleday & Co., 1968.

_____. *Memories, Dreams, Reflections.* New York: Pantheon Books, 1961.

_____. *Nietzsche's Zarathustra: Notes of the Seminar Given in 1934-1939* (Bollingen Series XCIX). 2 vols. Ed. James L. Jarrett. Princeton: Princeton University Press, 1988.

_____. *The Visions Seminars.* 2 vols. Zurich: Spring Publications, 1976.

_____. *The Wisdom of the Dream.* British TV film series. Produced and directed by Stephen Segaller. London, 1989.

Kirsch, Hildegarde. "Crossing the Ocean." *Psychological Perspectives,* vol. 6, no. 2 (Fall 1975).

Lasch, Christopher. *The Culture of Narcissism: American Life in an Age of Diminishing Expectations.* New York: Norton, 1978.

Lewis, C.S. *Reflections on the Psalms.* New York: Harcourt, Brace and World, 1958.

McGuire, William and Hull, R.F.C. *C.G. Jung Speaking* (Bollingen Series XCVII). Princeton: Princeton University Press, 1977.

McNemar, Q. *Psychological Statistics.* New York: John Wiley and Sons, Inc., 1962.

Moody Jr., Raymond A. *Life after Life.* New York: Bantam Books, 1975.

Myers, Henry. "Literature, Science and Democracy." In W.R. Keast and R.E. Streeter, *The Province of Prose.* New York: Harper and Row, 1956.

Nag Hammadi Library. Ed. James Robinson. San Francisco: Harper and Row, 1977.

Neumann, Erich. *The Child.* New York: C.G. Jung Foundation for Analytical Psychology, 1973.

———. "On the Moon and Matriarchal Consciousness." In *Fathers and Mothers: Five Papers on the Archetypal Background of Family Psychology.* Dallas: Spring Publications, 1973.

———. "Stages of Religious Experience and the Path of Depth Psychology." *Quadrant,* vol. 21, no. 1 (Spring 1988).

Otto, Rudolph. *The Idea of the Holy.* London: Oxford University Press, 1910.

Rilke, Rainer Maria. *Letters to a Young Poet.* Trans. Stephen Mitchell. New York: Vintage Books (Random House), 1986.

———. *The Selected Poetry of Rainer Maria Rilke.* Ed. and trans. Stephen Mitchell. New York: Vintage Books, 1984.

Ruby, Lois. *Two Truths in My Pocket.* New York: Viking Press, 1985.

Serbin, David. "In Conversation with Joseph B. Wheelwright." *Psychological Perspectives,* vol. 15, no. 2 (Fall 1984).

Sharp, Daryl. *Personality Types: Jung's Model of Typology.* Toronto: Inner City Books, 1987.

———. *The Survival Papers: Anatomy of a Midlife Crisis.* Toronto: Inner City Books, 1988.

Shattuck, Roger. "Why Not the Best?" *New York Review of Books,* April 28, 1983.

Sheldrake, Rupert. *A New Science of Life: The Hypothesis of Formative Causation.* Los Angeles: Jeremy P. Tarcher, 1981.

Silverman, Doris K. "What are Little Girls Made Of?" In *Psychoanalytic Psychology,* vol. 4, no. 4 (1987).

Singer, Isaac Bashevis. *Love and Exile.* New York: Strauss and Giroux, 1981.

Talbot, Michael. *Beyond the Quantum.* New York: Bantam New Age, 1988.

Tolstoy, Leo. *War and Peace.* Trans. Louise and Aylmer Maude. New York: Simon and Schuster, 1942.

Twain, Mark. *The Unabridged Mark Twain.* 2 vols. Ed. Lawrence Teacher. Philadelphia: Running Press, 1979.

von Franz, Marie-Louise. *C.G. Jung: His Myth in Our Time.* Trans. William H. Kennedy. New York: G.P. Putnam's Sons, 1975.

_____. "Forever Jung." In *Rolling Stone Magazine,* Nov. 21, 1985.

von Franz, Marie-Louise, in conversation with Fraser Boa. *The Way of the Dream.* Book and film. Toronto: Windrose Films, 1988.

Wehr, Gerhard. *Portrait of Jung: An Illustrated Biography.* Trans. W.A. Hargreaves. New York: Herder and Herder, 1971.

Wheelwright, Jane. *Feminine Spirit.* Unpublished manuscript.

Whitmont, Edward C. *The Symbolic Quest.* Princeton: Princeton University Press, 1969.

Wilhelm, Richard, trans. *The I Ching or Book of Changes* (Bollingen Series XIX). 3rd ed. Trans. into English by Cary F. Baynes. Princeton: Princeton University Press, 1967.

Woodman, Marion. *Addiction to Perfection: The Still Unravished Bride.* Toronto: Inner City Books, 1982.

_____. *The Pregnant Virgin: A Process of Psychological Transformation.* Toronto: Inner City Books, 1985.

Yeats, William Butler. *Collected Poems of W.B. Yeats.* New York: Macmillan, 1959.

Index

Abraham, 80-81, 101, 106, 108, 116-117
Adam, 38, 143-145
Adler, Gerhard, 99n, 119, 137, 163
Admetus, 157
Age of Reason, *see* Enlightenment
Aion (Jung), 38
Alcestis, 157
alchemy, 113, 161
Alcoholics Anonymous, 35
ambivalence, 53-54, 65
Anderson, Sherwood, 11, 84
androgyny, 145
Annunciation, 65, 144
anointing, 49-50
anti-Semitism, 106
Aphrodite, 147
apples, twisted, 84-85
archetype(s), 15, 28, 34, 47, 73, 79, 81, 126, 139
Ares, 56
Assumption of Mary, 99, 135-137

Badinter, Elizabeth, 149, 159n
Balaam, 65
bar mitzvah, 159
Barfield, Owen, 164
Barthes, Roland, 93n
Bauer, Jan, 35n
behaviorism, 94, 96
Berger, B., 92n
Bethany, 49-50
Blake, William, 42, 47
blood, 115, 117
body *(see also* instinct), 13, 61, 137-138
Bolen, Jean Shinoda, 35n
Brownmiller, Susan, 155

Buddhism, 11, 140

Campbell, Joseph, 146
Carlyle, Thomas, 58
Carotenuto, Aldo, 86n
census-taking, 97
Chanukah, 69
childhood, 44-45, 54, 69, 74-75, 87, 109-111, 115-116, 164
chosen, 102, 107, 111, 120-122, 138
Christ, 16-24, 26, 28, 38-59, 62, 65-69, 72, 75-80, 84, 87, 89-90, 104-105, 111, 115, 117, 120-122, 124-125, 129, 148, 164-165
Christian Archetype, The (Edinger), 38
Christian dispensation, 20, 108, 136, 144, 165
Christianity, 12, 28, 30, 32-34, 104-106, 108-109, 115, 121
Christmas, 68-69, 126
circumambulation, 13, 131
circumcision, 64
Clement of Alexandria, 53, 98
Communism, 158
confirmation, 159
compensation *(see also* opposites), 17-18, 27-29, 41, 45, 47, 60-69, 75, 120-122, 128, 135-136, 138, 153
complex(es), 118-120, 163
conflict, 41-43, 54, 57-59, 145, 155
conscience, 36, 38
consciousness, 35-36, 74-77, 102, 118, 136-137, 142-145, 155-158, 162-165
continuing incarnation, *see* incarnation
Copernicus, 73
Corbett, Lionel, 139n

171